PHILLIP COLLIER'S

MIXING NEW ORLEANS

COCKTAILS & LEGENDS

PHILLIP COLLIER'S

MIXING NEW ORLEANS

COCKTAILS & LEGENDS

Text by Jennifer Adams with photography by Michael Terranova
Foreword by Wayne Curtis

PHILBEAU PUBLISHING, INC.
NEW ORLEANS

Absinthe advertisement from "This Week in New Orleans" magazine, March 12, 1949.

Designed by:
Phillip Collier Designs: Phillip Collier, Dean Cavalier

Cover Design:
Phillip Collier Dean Cavalier

Cover Images:
Mint Julep photograph by Michael Terranova
Revelers at the Court of Two Sisters, circa 1940's, Historic New Orleans Collection, accession no.1974.25.2.68

Back Cover image:
Absinthe glass photograph by Michael Terranova

First edition printed by Harvey Hauser Printing Co.
New Orleans, LA

Manufactured in the United States of America

Library of Congress
Cataloguing-in-Publication data available.

ISBN 10: 0-9796977-0-0
ISBN 13: 978-0-9796977-0-8
SAN: 854-1469

10 9 8 7 6 5 4 3 2 1

Philbeau Publishing, Inc.
365 Canal Street
New Orleans, LA 70130

Dedicated to

HUGH ALVIN RICKS

1938 to 2005

Artist, Renaissance man and my dear friend.
For me, the greatest loss of Hurricane Katrina

&

ANN C. ROGERS

Founder of Tales of the Cocktail who encouraged me to do this book.

"Absinthe House, New Orleans", a 1946 oil painting by Guy Pène du Bois.

Photograph of a West End saloon on New Orleans' Lake Pontchartrain shore taken by George Francois Mugnier at the beginning of the 20th Century.

TABLE OF CONTENTS

FOREWORD

The man sitting next to me at the bar seemed uncommonly conversant in the arcane history of bitters.

I had flown to New Orleans in January 2005 while researching a book on the history of rum and rum cocktails. A couple of hours after I arrived, I stopped into Arnaud's French 75 bar — a place I'd picked more or less at random - for a cocktail before dinner. I started chatting with a quiet, tall man sitting next to me and our talk soon turned to bitters. A lively discussion ensued.

At one point he nonchalantly reached in his pocket and pulled out five eye-dropper-sized bottles of bitters — one of Angostura, and four concoctions he had made himself based on obscure and antique recipes.

This made a large impression on me. By the end of the evening, perhaps guided by the enlivening effects of finely crafted cocktails, I had the indelible impression that everyone in New Orleans — residents and visitors alike — carried around little bottles of their own homemade bitters.

I have since been informed this is not the case. As it turned out, the man next to me was Robert Hess, a well-known cocktail expert from Seattle, who happened to be in town, like me, for the opening of the Museum of the American Cocktail exhibit at the Pharmacy Museum.

Photograph of Tujague's Bar during the 1940's.

In fact, a great many experts in the history of cocktails had descended on the city that week. Over the next few days I fell in with them, roaming the streets and studying drink much as an art student might amble through Venice in the company of learned professors. I took notes and absorbed much, both in the cerebral and corporeal senses. I drank Sazeracs at Tujaques, Vieux Carrés at the Carousel Bar, Swizzles at the Swizzle Stick Bar, Pimm's Cups at the sublime Napoleon House, and memorably minty Mojitos at the Marigny Brasserie.

This was not a lesson in history nor a lesson in contemporary culture, but something pleasantly in-between — which I soon learned is the place where New Orleans excels. I can think of few cities where the past and present are on such friendly terms.

This can be observed almost everywhere: in restaurants, in neighborhood clubs, in street parades, in the architecture. You never find forced displays of "our traditions", concocted by well-meaning civic boosters. New Orleans is not like most other cities, where history is put in depressing little history zoos, and visitors are invited to gawk and feed the history some stale biscuits. The past is animated and healthy here, and, perhaps, even a little pushy. That's as it should be.

Phillip Collier, Jennifer Adams, and Michael Terranova have done a great service for all of us who enjoy tippling in this dusky zone between past and present. Mixing New Orleans celebrates the city's rich past, putting in the cocktail shaker a full measure of history, a half-measure of legend, and a dash of recipes and guidance, producing a nicely balanced volume that serves well as a guide to genteel drinking — that is, drinking as it was meant to be done. (As Robert Hess put it during our chat at Arnaud's French 75: "Drinking to get drunk is like having sex to get pregnant.")

Bourbon Street, with its lurid Hand Grenades and multi-hued alcoholic slurpees may capture the imagination of the misinformed, but New Orleans is far more sophisticated than that. *Mixing New Orleans* is the perfect launch point to begin an exploration of that far richer culture.

After another trip to New Orleans — during which I attended Tales of the Cocktail for the first, but not the last time — I started wondering why I didn't live here. I couldn't come up with an adequate answer to that question, so upon returning to New England, I explained to my wife that we had to pack up and move south.

Happily, she agreed. (I'm pleased to report, with complete accuracy, that drink drove me to New Orleans.) We arrived here less than a year after Katrina abruptly rearranged the city's life and culture, but what impressed us then and continues to do so is the utter resilience of the place. The roots of the city's culture run deep. The past continues to nurture the future.

And that's certainly worth drinking to.

Wayne Curtis,
Author of *And a Bottle of Rum: A History of the New World in Ten Cocktails*
New Orleans, Louisiana
June 4, 2007

PREFACE

The book you are holding now began in 1996 when Paul Alker of Harvey Press approached me. As a local printer, Paul knew the importance of appealing to his New Orleans clientele. He contacted my graphic design studio to create a promotional campaign that would convey the high level of his company's printing capabilities.

His only request was that the campaign use New Orleans as a theme. Together we decided that a series of over-sized brochures, featuring beautiful color photographs, typography and design, would not only highlight his company's craftsmanship and printing techniques, but would also entertain and educate people. Paul and I discussed New Orleans and what it meant to be from here and what it truly meant to live here. Naturally, the subjects of food, beverage and hospitality came to the forefront and I proposed we do four books on classic bars, restaurants, hotels, and stores. *Local Libations*, the first brochure of the series, was born.

A visual history of saloons, cocktails, and locally produced beers, I wanted *Local Libations* to evoke nostalgia in design, picture and prose. I recruited my friend Michael Terranova for the photography, and over the next year, I accompanied him to one bar after another, shooting cocktails and eves, absinthe spoons and wrought iron. Months of research followed. I scoured out-of-print books for the text and the archives of the Historic New Orleans Collection for photographs and art. I also sought out collectors of beer and bar memorabilia, and just as it seemed we were nearing a cohesive point to begin assembling it all, Harvey Press was sold to an out-of-town printer.

Our hard work began to crumble. We were informed that the new owners felt alcohol had little to do with promoting a printing company. Yet Paul prevailed and after much time and effort managed to convince them that this one project had merit. Our subsequent brochures would never see fruition, but *Local Libations* would proceed, only smaller than expected. Five hundred copies were printed, and they were distributed to a few of the Harvey Press customers, my friends and family and a few clients of my design firm. The rest found a box, which found a shelf, and, with a sense of sadness, that was it.

I had licked my wounds on the issue and forgotten about it until this year when Ann Rogers approached me with an idea. As founder of Tales of the Cocktail, Ann understood the importance of liquid culture — especially in New Orleans, the so-called birthplace of the cocktail. Her festival, now in its fifth year, celebrates the history of cocktails and libations, bartenders and drinking spots around the city. The whole event is geared toward toasting food and beverage and the impact it has on all of our lives. She inquired about *Local Libations*, what had happened to it, and the possibility of resurrecting it to launch at the 2007 Tales of the Cocktail festival this July.

I was more than skeptical. Harvey Press was ravaged by Hurricane Katrina, and even if we had the files — which we didn't — the oversized format of the book and use of extra ink colors and varnishes were not affordable for commercial sale. Also, *Local Libations* was much more to me than

Pages shown from the book "Local Libations" lamenting the loss of hand-chipped ice for cocktails at Galatoires.

had been printed. There were countless bars that deserved pages, countless stories left that needed to be told. And then there was the deadline. Publish the whole thing by July? This was March. To make matters worse, my wife Cindie and I were dealing daily with subcontractors and mired in the process of rebuilding our home, which was flooded in the hurricane. In addition to living amongst constant construction and frustration, plus keeping up with the workload of other projects for my studio, I would have three months to triple the size, photograph new drinks and bars, and find a writer.

I mentally paced back and forth on the idea for a week when Michael agreed to jump in the deep end with me. Through Ann, we met Jennifer Adams, then the associate editor of *Nightclub & Bar* magazine. We asked her if she thought there was enough time to rewrite the book from scratch. We had a stipulation that this time the book needed to include everything we were forced to sacrifice the first time — plus some. That stipulation demanded entirely fresh text on old subjects and new.

Jennifer loved the idea and the opportunity. She transitioned to a role as contributing editor for the magazine, drove down to New Orleans, and dove in with us. So it was that the four of us got to work — a lot of work.

Bringing this idea to print means a great deal to me and to everyone who has been a part of the 10-year process along the way. New Orleans is a town of great spirit, and much of that is attributed to our food and beverage industry. The insane deadline we faced would have been insurmountable had it not been for the generosity, patience and excitement for the project on the part of all of the establishments, companies, bartenders, owners and friendly patrons who were involved. Thank you all so very much, and I hope you enjoy *Mixing New Orleans Cocktails & Legends.*

May your glasses be ever full,
Phillip Collier,
New Orleans, Louisiana
May 22, 2007

Acknowledgements

Phillip Collier, Michael Terranova and Jennifer Adams would like to thank:

First and foremost, Dean Cavalier of Phillip Collier Designs. It was Dean who took Phillip's ideas in the form of sketchy, illegible layouts, Jennifer's constantly changing text and Michael's photographs and brought them all together in visual harmony on these pages. Thanks as well to designers Scott Carroll and Elizabeth Conway, food stylist Martha Torres, illustrator Mark Andresen, and Stan Dupree, Bob Butz, and the late Eddie Williams of Alliance Pre-Press for help with the visual portions of *Local Libations* that were used in this book.

There is no place like home, and our families felt the strain of this book as much as we did at times. Thank you to Riki Collier for her fine work compiling the appendix and writing last minute photo captions, to Cindie Collier for cutting lemon twists and finding props for the numerous drink shots, and to James Collier, Kelly Cavalier, and Linda Henderson for proofreading the final text. Thank you to Cathy Adams for all the editing that never seemed to end.

From their attics, basements and bar shelves full of countless treasures, we would like to thank Steve Latter, Ted and Ellen Brennan, Al Kleindienst, Cary Bonnecaze, B. J. Bordelon III and B. Raymond Bordelon for providing much of the memorabilia of yesteryear.

We sought a tremendous amount of advice and suggestions for this project. Those who deserve

our debt of gratitude include Kit Wohl, Richard Sexton, John Magill, Rusty Harris, Ben Gersh, Peggy Scott Laborde, Liz Williams of the Southern Food & Beverage Museum, Robert Hess, Billie Cox, and Dr. Richard Gruber of The Ogden Museum of Southern Art. Jennifer would also like to thank everyone she interviewed, relentlessly questioned and daily sought out for moral support including Colette Guste, Melvin Rodrigue, Claire Creppel, George Eckert, Katy Casbarian, Chris Hannah, Kenneth Holditch, Stanley Schwam, Kevin Richards, Ben Gersh, Cary Bonnecaze, Steve Latter, Andrea Thornton, Angela Haber, Sal Impastato, Joe Razzano, Rey Velaquez, Mike Reese, Shelly Waguespack, Bonnie Warren, Alana Brennan, Joe Gendusa, Sandy Shilstone, Victoria Matassa, Jeff Adams, Tom Adams, Lindsay Moylan, Chris Eissman and the staff of *Nightclub & Bar* magazine. She would also like to say thanks to the people and establishments that gave her a place to stay while she was in New Orleans including the Harrah's Hotel, Cary Alden and the Omni Royal Orleans and the Impastato family of the Napoleon House.

A special thanks also goes to Sally Stassi of the Historic New Orleans Collection, Judith D. Smith and Charlene Bennette of the Louisiana State Library, and Irene Wainwright of the New Orleans Public Library for the help in securing archival materials used in the book. We would like to thank all of the staff members, owners and operators of the places we invaded to photograph.

We also have an extended "we owe you one" to one very important segment of our team — a toast to Ann C. Rogers and Tales of the Cocktail. From her role as the initial spark that fueled all of us to come together on this project, to her efforts promoting the book, before and after publication, both Ann Rogers and her festival have been a vital source of energy for this book. Tales of the Cocktail is an annual culinary event celebrating the history of the cocktail in New Orleans. In its fifth year, Tales of the Cocktail has attracted thousands of visitors to attend the event, many culinary and cocktail celebrities as presenters and hosts of the event and several top spirit brands and national magazines among other well-known companies as sponsors for Tales of the Cocktail.

In 2006, for Tales of the Cocktail's fourth year, Ann formed the New Orleans Culinary and Cultural Preservation Society to preserve New Orleans' dining and drinking history, raise funds for the hospitality industry and produce the annual event.

Ann and her employees at Tales of the Cocktail gave their time on this project freely and without complaint or compensation. They all do a tremendous amount for the city of New Orleans, and we are thankful and proud to launch *Phillip Collier's Mixing New Orleans Cocktails & Legends* as a small part of this year's Tales of the Cocktail Festival.

Finally, we want to thank Marvin Allen of the Carousel Piano Bar and Lounge, who at the last minute was enlisted to be our resident mixologist and drink recipe consultant. To anyone we might have overlooked in our insane scramble to make it to publication, we thank you and hope you forgive us for the mistake.

Here's to you,

Phillip Collier, Michael Terranova and Jennifer Adams

INTRODUCTION

They say that if you don't learn from history you are doomed to repeat it. Well, it is characteristic of New Orleans' history that if you hear a good story you are doomed to repeat it as well. Only, you add a dash of exaggeration, an ounce of embellishment for flavor and a stir. You have a recipe for repetition — for two hundred years or more.

As I researched and wrote the brief histories in this book, it was a goal to find the scraps authors have passed up publishing for lack of proof. In some instances I succeeded in finding small treasures not frequently published, in others I was resigned to retell stories that we have all grown to know by heart. Our small team endeavored to highlight the classics of New Orleans. The classic people, classic places, classic stories, and, of course, classic cocktails. Some of the pages and people who graciously offered up information did so with New Orleans' attitude. It's not so important the exact day and time. Cold hard fact is worn down over hundreds of years of nostalgic retelling, and what survives and what remains are the feelings and emotions each legend evoked. These are the sentiments that stitch each tale into the oral tapestry of history forever.

There really is no city like New Orleans. That statement is not a pretty piece of propaganda for the visitor brochures or a slogan to sell more airline tickets. The truth of it is visible everywhere — seared into each balcony's iron scrollwork with every climbing degree of the tropical summer heat.

New Orleans toasts her accomplishments with her faults, and, like a true lady, she is a constantly evolving secret to be discovered. A petrified forest of architecture and ambiance — it is a place where simply stepping into an open bar can spirit you away from the rest of the world for an afternoon or a lifetime.

All it takes is sliding onto a worn barstool and easing the soul with a Sazerac and a great tale from the bartender polishing glasses.

The bars of New Orleans are chalices of history, big enough to hold us all, captivated as we sip, spellbound as we learn. There is history carved literally and figuratively into every faded wall. There are bartenders who have poured

For many years female customers were not allowed in the Sazerac Bar except for "Fat Tuesday" (Mardi Gras Day) when they were invited to "storm" the bar, as seen in this picture. Seymour Weiss, the manager of the Roosevelt Hotel, ended the century-old prohibition against women in the early 1950s.

the same brands for fifty years, pacing the same worn stone space behind the bar. These people are the keepers of myth and truth. Their stories are as mixed and indistinguishable on a rainy afternoon as the liquor from the juice — once shaken, once told.

It must be a real honor to be from New Orleans. It is an emotion I will never know, but it is something that I hope to learn more about in my lifetime. I am grateful for this city's lessons on historic preservation, random revelry and tenacious spirit. I am grateful that I was allowed to be a part of this project, and I hope you enjoy reading this book as much as I enjoyed writing it.

All the best,
Jennifer Adams,
Oxford Mississippi
May 22, 2007

During absinthe's vogue in the late 19th and early 20th century, it was dispensed in bars from Paris to New Orleans in doses. Shown here is a French absinthe topette with etched doser marks that showed the bar owner how many doses his patron had consumed.

I

LIQUID HISTORIES

Alcohol helps to shape each tavern it lives inside, our culture overall and the legends we pass down generation after generation. These liquid histories trace the origins of New Orleans' native spirits and the cocktails and establishments they have inspired.

COLLOSOL
MANGANESE
OIL SWEET BIRCH
DODGE & OLCOTT
SPINTRATE
CHEMICAL CO
EMPTY CAPSULES

PEYCHAUD'S BITTERS

There are many stories surrounding the origin of the cocktail and its name. New Orleans' own folklore contains the following account — which begins with Antoine Amedee Peychaud's arrival in New Orleans circa 1795. Fleeing from his homeland of Santo Domingo and the strife and slaughter of the slave revolt in 1793, Peychaud was one amongst the tremendous number of French-speaking refugees who relocated to New Orleans — bringing with them their Caribbean roots, rhythms and recipes. It is believed that one recipe in particular, Peychaud's own bitters, was a family secret.

Peychaud opened and ran an apothecary shop on Royal Street around the third decade of the 19th century, and, like many other pharmacists, he experimented with fermented spirits. In the early 1800s, there was a fine line between spirits and medicine, and alcohol was once a redeemer of ills before it was branded during Prohibition as ill itself.

Antoine Peychaud was also a Mason and a member of the Concorde Blue Lodge, and his shop became an after-hours destination for his brothers in the order. On these nights, Peychaud would blend brandy and his bitters together and serve the concoction in the large end of an egg cup. Peychaud thus created what is considered by some to be the first American cocktail. The egg cup itself was double-ended, and its resembalance to a present day jigger was possibly more than mere coincidence. In all likelihood, it was the common bartending tool's predecessor.

As for the actual appellation, "cocktail," — it was derived in part to egregious mispronunciation of the original French word for egg cup, "coquetier." People, especially the new Americans, slandered the pronunciation, calling them "cocktays" and finally, "cocktails."

Above: Antoine Amedee Peychaud ran his pharmacy out of this building in the French Quarter, now 437 Royal Street.
Left: The New Orleans Pharmacy Museum offers a glimpse of a time when pharmacists worked a fine line between being doctors and bartenders. An old Peychaud Bitters bottle is visible in the foreground.

Peychaud's Manhattan

The Roaring Twenties era inspired very animated art, and one of the most appreciated names of the time was illustrator John Held, Jr. Held's *Life* magazine covers captured the flapper culture with such panache that his work became a symbol of the time period overall.

In 1935, Peychaud's published a cocktail book with recipes and illustrations by Held. Under an illustration of a man and a woman in the throes of sheer cocktail-induced revelry, Held had a recipe for mixing a cocktail called the Peychaud's Manhattan. He advised "East-side-west-side and all around the town to be sung by a mixed quartette," following the mixing instructions.

Cracked ice
1 ½ oz. Sazerac Rye®
¾ oz. sweet vermouth
2 dashes Peychaud's Bitters®
Maraschino cherry

Mix rye, vermouth and bitters, with cracked ice in a mixing glass. Strain into a chilled cocktail glass. Garnish with maraschino cherry. (We have substituted rye for blended whiskey in Held's original recipe.)

***Right:** Peychaud's special bitters was bottled long before the Sazerac Company of New Orleans acquired the rights in 1970, but during that year, the Sazerac Company became the sole maker and distributor of the legendary bitters.*

PEYCHAUD'S
AROMATIC COCKTAIL BITTER
DIPLOMA OF HONOR
AWARDED AT
GRAND EXHIBITION OF ALTONA-GERMA
Bitters
equal for
cocktails
every bar
prominence
L'amer Peychaud
sur passe´
om atique
les cock-
usage dans
meilleurs
ST. LOUIS 1904
GOLD MEDAL
NEW ORLEANS 1884-1885
BRONZE MEDAL ATLANTA, GA. 1895
GOLD MEDAL ST. LOUIS 1904 -- GOLD MEDAL PORTLAND, ORE. 1905
HIGHEST AWARD, JAMESTOWN 1907
PRODUCED FROM
THE ORIGINAL FORMULA FOR
L. E. JUNG AND WOLFF CO.
803 JEFFERSON HWY. NEW ORLEANS, LA 70121
35% ALCOHOL BY VOLUME
CONTENTS 5 FL. OZS. (148 ml)

SAZERAC

THE SAZERAC

While the people of New Orleans had begun to enjoy "cocktails" in the mid 1800s, they were not yet enjoying them in bars. Drinking establishments were then known as coffee houses, many of which were named after precious stones in the 1850s. This time in the city's history became referred to as "the glittering decade" of coffee houses. In 1851, the Gem opened on Royal, so named due to the fact that the Ruby, the Pearl and the Diamond were already taken. As things progressed, the names became livelier, and documentation from the City Directory of 1859 lists some 204 coffee houses in business — among them, the "Golden Age," the "Veteran Drummer," the "Continental," the "Iron Horse" and the "Merchants Exchange."

The Merchants Exchange Coffee House was originally located on the corner, at 16 Royal and 13 Exchange Alley, but in the year of 1850 owner Sewell Taylor moved to 15 - 17 Royal Street and opened a liquor store, hiring Thomas H. Handy as his clerk. At the same time, Aaron Bird purchased the Old Merchants Exchange Coffee House and changed the name to read the Sazerac Coffee House. What he offered those inside was a sip or several of the era's popular French brandy, Sazerac-de-Forge et fils, and a dash of Peychaud's Bitters. The catalysts continued, and Antoine Peychaud's curious drink began to morph from liquid in an egg cup to the legend it is today.

The Sazerac Coffee House was owned and operated from 1853 until 1895 by Aaron Bird, but it is actually the subsequent proprietor, John B. Schiller, who is often credited with heavily promoting the Sazerac cocktail. His strict recipe demanded Sazerac-de-Forge et fils brandy with a dash of Peychaud's Bitters, and his venue and its signature libation were so popular that some sources claim Schiller may have made in excess of a quarter of a million dollars in his lifetime.

The final say in Sazerac, in reference to both the drink and the venue, was not yet settled. After his death in 1869, Schiller's Sazerac Coffee House was taken over by Thomas H. Handy, who was at that time working for Schiller as a clerk. In 1873, Handy replaced the French brandy with American rye whiskey, dropped the word "coffee" from the building's front, and added a dash of romance in the form of absinthe to the drink's base.

Handy's new Sazerac House began serving America's new Sazerac cocktail.

Left: Bar menus shaped like popular cocktails of the day were common at the Roosevelt Hotel in the mid 1900s.
Above: Exchange Alley around the turn of the 20th century.

This picture, taken sometime in the 1930s, captures an apt and ready bar staff at the Sazerac Bar. At that time, the bar was located on the corner of Carondelet and Gravier in the Central Business District, removed from its original spot on Royal Street and Exchange Alley. In the mid 1900s, the city's signature sip was served for only 20 cents on the dollar. After Prohibition, the Sazerac Bar moved once more and settled in the Roosevelt Hotel.

Whiskies
TNA 25
SON
"THAT'S ALL"
HI-BALL
15
RTIN COGNAC
V.S.O.P.
30

SAZERAC®
RYE
STRAIGHT
RYE WHISKEY
ALC 45% BY VOL (90 PROOF)

The Sazerac

The Sazerac is the city's most enduring and endearing drink. Simple, classic and timeless, it is a trinity of New Orleans' oldest spirits.

Crushed ice
2 oz. Sazerac Rye®
2 dashes Peychaud's Bitters®
1/4 oz. simple syrup
2 dashes Herbsaint®
Ice cubes
Lemon Peel

Chill 2 old fashioned glasses with crushed ice. Empty one glass, and add Sazerac, Pechaud's Bitters and simple syrup along with a few ice cubes. Stir well and set aside. Empty the other glass and add Herbsaint. Swirl glass to coat thoroughly, then pour out excess Herbsaint. Strain mixture into this glass. Twist lemon peel over drink and serve.

***Left:** In 1999, the Sazerac Company began producing Sazerac Rye whiskey again. The rebirth of the brand meant that the Sazerac Company owned the trio of classic New Orleans ingredients associated with the city's official drink.*

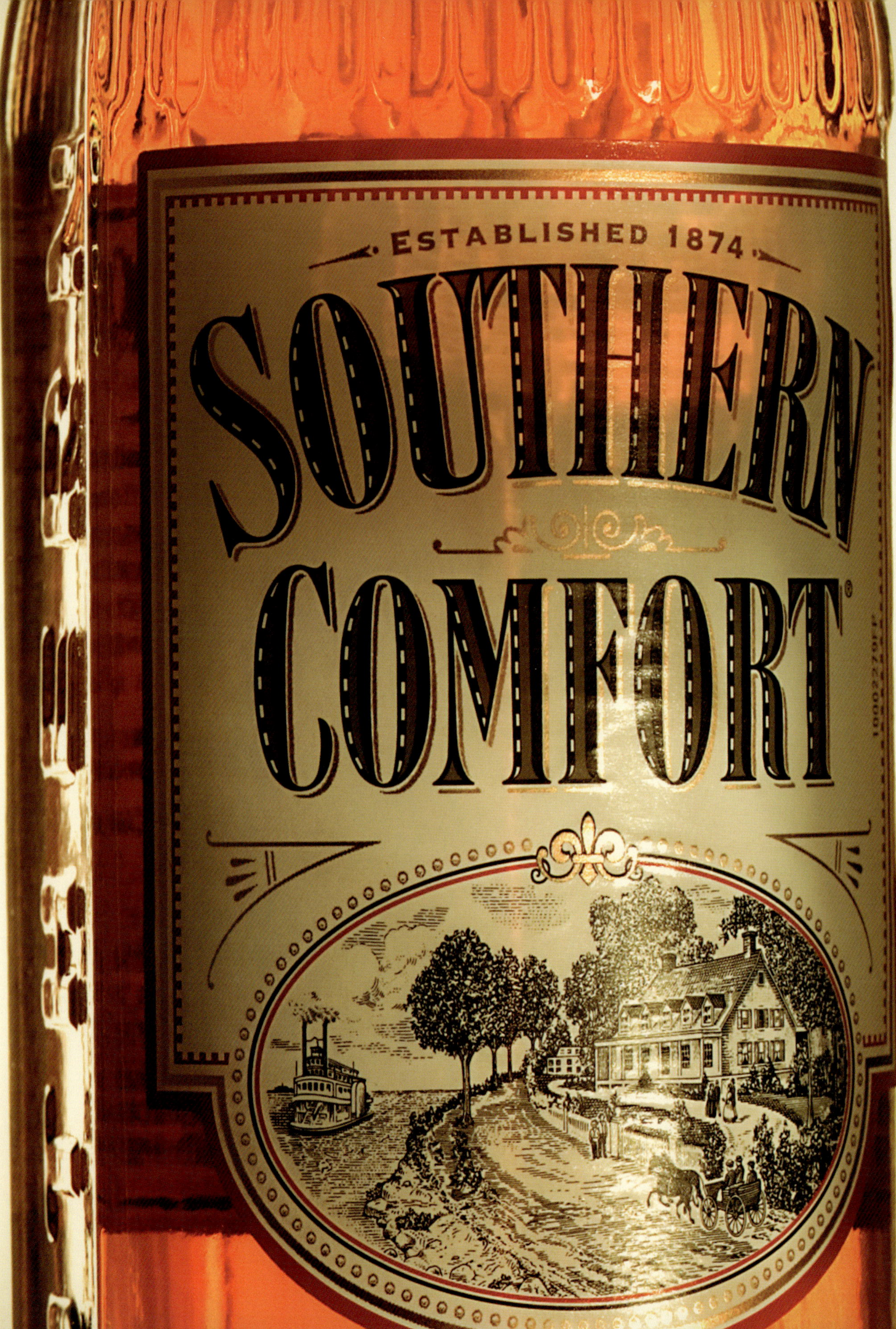
ESTABLISHED 1874
SOUTHERN
COMFORT®

SOUTHERN COMFORT

In the last days of the 1800s and the ones just following the century's turn, raised and rowdy toasts would prove to produce legendary friendships and even more celebrated liquid relationships. Those were the days when Mr. Jack Daniel literally met M. W. Heron's sense of southern comfort.

Small batch and single malt varieties that we covet and wax prolific about today are a far cry from the liquor pouring out of Old Bourbon, Kentucky in the 19th century.

Whiskey was as coarse as the swarthy men who drank it, and, as such, cultivating a refined taste for the amber liquors was nearly impossible since no two barrels ever tasted the same.

A New Orleans bartender by the name of M. W. Heron was employed at McCauley's Tavern off of Bourbon Street when he began stirring lemon, lime, cherry and orange into the fickle whiskeys in an attempt to bring some semblance of continuity on the palate. Moroccan cinnamon, exotic vanillas and other dark spices were added, and in 1889 Heron's claims of "None Genuine but Mine" and "Two per customer. No Gentleman would ask for more," were slapped on every bottle of his tasty "Cuffs & Buttons" — so named because his most fearsome competitor was then producing "Hats & Tails." In 1904, Heron earned a gold medal at the World's Fair in St. Louis — and in an ironic, historical twist — congratulations from a new friend, Mr. Jack Daniel.

"Cuffs & Buttons" was re-christened "Southern Comfort," and thankfully so, since "a Cuffs & Buttons & Coke" is somewhat of a mouthful.

A Currier & Ives illustration was added to the front label in 1934, and its real-life inspiration is located just miles from New Orleans in West Point a la Hache on the Mississippi River. Woodland Plantation in Plaquemines Parish, Louisiana is the only plantation home between New Orleans and the Gulf of Mexico that is still open to the public. It is currently owned by the Creppel family, who also own the Columns Hotel on St. Charles Avenue.

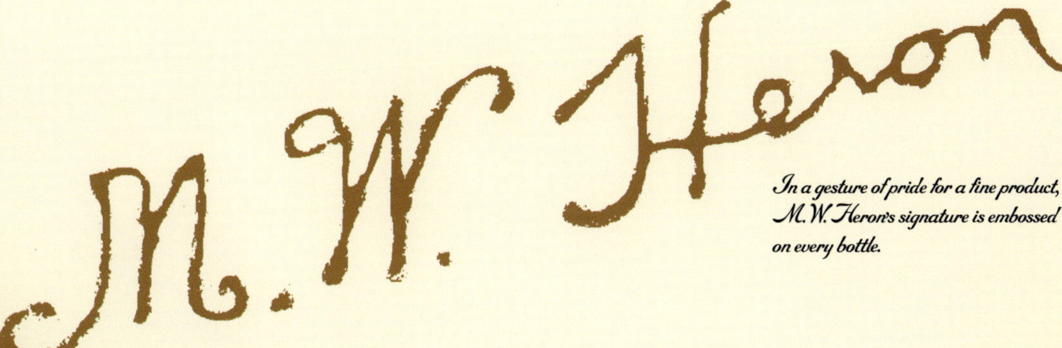

In a gesture of pride for a fine product, M. W. Heron's signature is embossed on every bottle.

Scarlett O'Hara

The Scarlett O'Hara cocktail history is as changing as the heroine's moods in the movie, *Gone with the Wind*. Some claim the drink was invented in 1939 as a tie-in to the film in which Rhett and Scarlett honeymoon in New Orleans, while other sources — the less romantic ones — demand it was created later as a ploy to sell more cranberry juice in the 1950's. Like Vivien Leigh's character, the cocktail is marked by both its southern sweetness and its ability to cause trouble after repeated encounters.

Ice Cubes
1 ½ oz. Southern Comfort®
1 ½ oz. cranberry juice
One squeeze of lime

Combine all ingredients with ice in a tall glass. Mix well and garnish with a lime wheel.

Left: Detail of Wooland Plantation engraving by Alfred Wald that appeared in "Every Saturday," May 20, 1871.

French Absinthe poster circa 1902.

ABSINTHE

It went by many nicknames, among them the "the green fairy" for its coloring and "the black death" for its licorice taste. It was the opiate of choice in America — the accepted vice of society, both high and low. Like the chartreuse snake sliding through the Garden of Eden, absinthe would earn a misunderstood and sordid reputation before it was demonized completely and banned from the United States in 1912.

Absinthe's first function, however, was far less romantic and illicit than the artistic rendezvous history would repeat long after its American heyday. A mixture of anise, coriander, fennel and wormwood, absinthe was originally used to settle a disturbed stomach. Produced from these common herbs at the base of the Swiss Alps, the mystic green liquid's popularity swam into the French consciousness due to several contributing factors.

In the mid 1800s, the Algerians in Northern Africa were fighting a war with French aid. Absinthe was used to cleanse suspect water and to reduce the prevalence of dysentery among the soldiers, and when the war ended in the late 1800s many returned to France, fresh from the fight with an acquired taste for the previously required herbal digestive.

During this time there were also problems in the wine industry in Europe. Two years of insect infestation ravaged crops, adding to absinthe's appeal.

Above: Farmers harvesting wormwood to make absinthe.
Right : Vintage bottle of Pernod Fils Absinthe – the 60 degree content equals 120 proof.

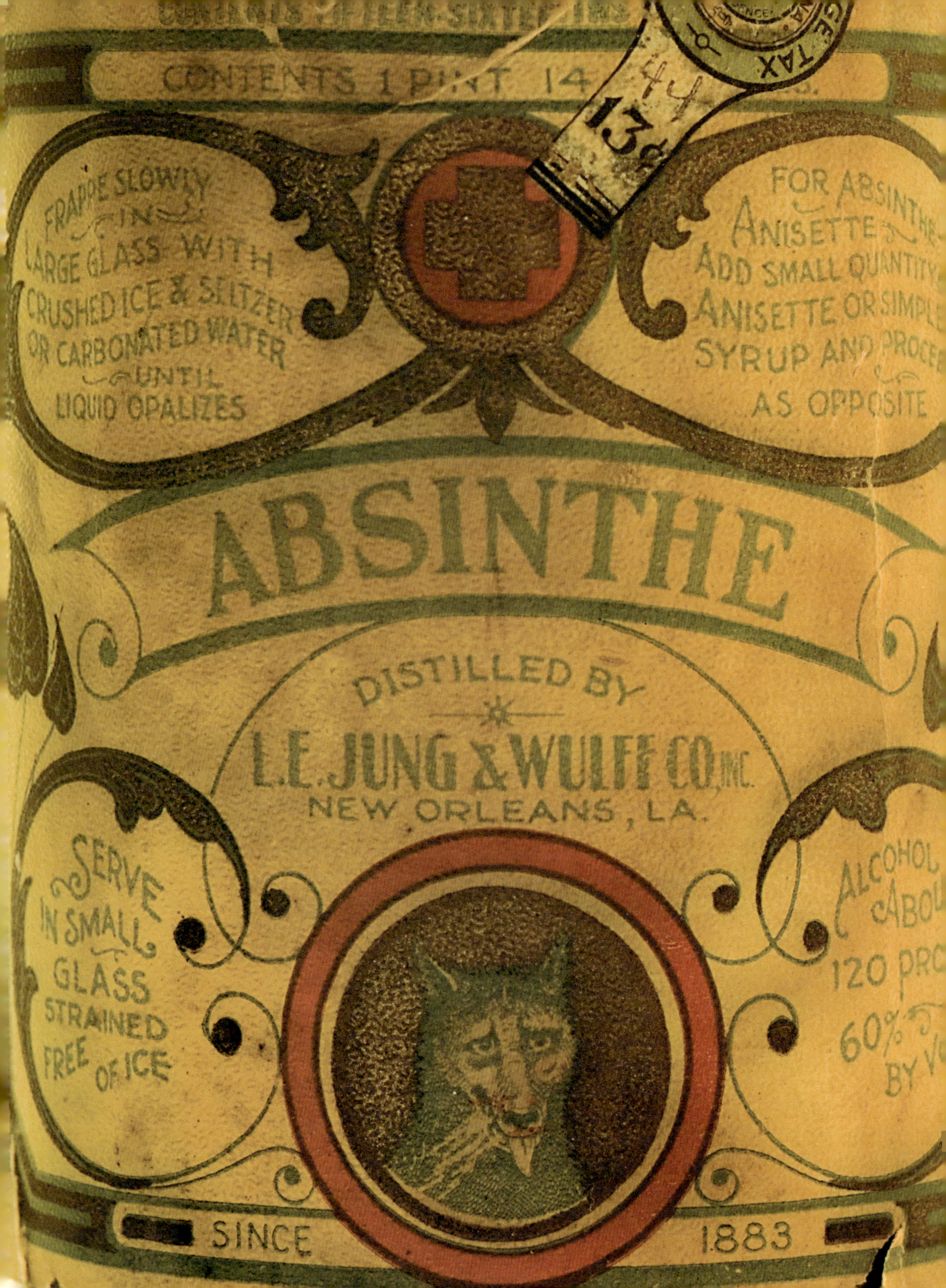
CONTENTS 1 PINT 14
FRAPPE SLOWLY IN LARGE GLASS WITH CRUSHED ICE & SELTZER OR CARBONATED WATER UNTIL LIQUID OPALIZES
FOR ABSINTHE ANISETTE ADD SMALL QUANTITY ANISETTE OR SIMPLE SYRUP AND PROCE
AS OPPOSITE
ABSINTHE
DISTILLED BY
L.E. JUNG & WULFF CO. INC.
NEW ORLEANS, LA.
SERVE IN SMALL GLASS STRAINED FREE OF ICE
ALCOHOL ABOU
120 PRO
60% BY V
SINCE
1883

Absinthe made in New Orleans under the label of L.E. Jung and Wulff was distilled at 317-319 Magazine Street between 1883 and 1912. There were several other distillers of absinthe in the city at this time and they all formed the New Orleans Absinthe Manufacturers Association. The bottle pictured here was discovered by a local collector at a flea market and is thought to be the only existing example of a Jung and Wulff Absinthe bottle with the actual paper labels still attached.

While its widespread popularity and availability in Europe was due to extraneous events, absinthe's debut in America was largely due to Henri Louis Pernod. Pernod began producing and exporting absinthe to the American cities of Chicago, San Francisco and New York in 1805. His emerald city for absinthe consumption, however, was New Orleans.

Hypnotic in its vogue, high-society form of deviance, absinthe wound itself around the cultured artistic in New Orleans just as it had done in the Bohemian Art movements of Paris. After all, New Orleans already answered to the nickname "the Little Paris of America," and in the Crescent City absinthe found its largest following with Pernod exporting millions of liters a year.

Coffee houses such as The Old Absinthe House on Bourbon Street sprang to life, and a day's end became the "green hour" or "l'heure verte," in honor of its new signature sip. Absinthe fountains dropped fat drops of water over slotted spoons carrying sugar cubes, and when the sugary water slid through the spoon it created the desired "louche," or milky effect, changing from green to slightly yellow. A true artist's accomplice and an aspiring drunk's artifice, absinthe's reign was soured by its rampant popularity. Inferior imitations were produced, thujone — the active sedative ingredient in wormwood — was accused of causing hallucinations, and nations around the world began to ban the haunted liquor.

From the ban in 1912, it would take some 22 years until Herbsaint arrived. J. M. Legendre began producing it after Prohibition, utilizing skills and experience in making actual absinthe he had learned in France during World War I. His "Legendre Absinthe" product was unique since, unlike pastis, it was the first substitute for absinthe. J.M. Legendre began releasing his Legendre Absinthe New Orleans in 1934. The Alcohol Control Bureau was upset by the name, and although it contained no wormwood, they forced Legendre to change the product's appellation. Legendre Absinthe became Legendre Herbsaint, with the original recipe remaining intact.

Today, you would be hard pressed to find a bar without a bottle of Herbsaint behind it, and if you know where to look and whom to beseech, you could find an authentic glass of absinthe in the city as well. You can find pretty much anything in New Orleans if you know where to look and whom to ask.

Right: Years of slowly dripping water from the spigots eroded the Old Absinthe House marble base fountains' foundations. Physical proof of times passing, the history lies in what you don't see.

Shown here in 1903, The Old Absinthe House was a rendezvous point for those in search of artistic muses and afternoon gossip.

Absinthe Frappé

*Cracked ice**
2 oz. Herbsaint®
1/2 tsp. simple syrup or one sugar cube
2 oz. water

Into an old fashioned glass filled with cracked ice, pour Herbsaint, simple syrup and water or slowly drip the water over the sugar cube placed on an absinthe spoon. Stir gently. Strain into a well chilled old fashioned glass.

**Always use cracked ice not crushed. Crushed ice will dilute the subtle taste of the frappé.*

***Right:** The Sazerac Company acquired the J. M. Legendre Company in 1949, and with the purchase came the rights to the brand Herbsaint.*

HERBSAINT®
NINETY PROOF
Liqueur d'Anis
AS SERVED IN THE OLD ABSINTHE HOUSE
FAMOUS NEW ORLEANS LANDMARK
The Spirit of New Orleans
ALC 45% BY VOL (90 PROOF)
AND BOTTLED BY LEGENDRE CO., FRANKFORT, KY

THE FAMOUS
RAMOS'
GIN Fizz
SOLD EXCLUSIVELY AT ROOSEVELT BARS
NEW ORLEANS
50¢

In 1935, the Roosevelt Hotel trademarked the Ramos Gin Fizz as its official drink. The hotel often displayed their drink menus in a cutout form of a popular cocktail. The one shown here dates back to 1947, when the highly demanded fizz was priced at half a dollar.

RAMOS GIN FIZZ

The first Ramos Gin Fizz was created by Henry Ramos in 1888, at his bar in the Meyer's Table d'Hotel Internationale, on the corner of Gravier and Carondelet Streets.

The secret recipe called for mixing together gin, super-fine caster sugar, orange-flower water, lemon juice, lime juice, cream, seltzer water and egg whites. The trick to the cocktail was in the vigorous and lively nature of the shake, and the frothy outcome was heaven on a hot, humid summer's day. The creamy texture of this gin fizz furthered its popularity as an early century hangover cure as well.

Ramos later moved to the Imperial Cabinet Saloon along with his prized drink, serving it exclusively in that bar. Stories abound that the drink and the bar were so popular during the 1915 Carnival season that Ramos was forced to employ dozens of "shaker boys" just to adequately agitate all of the cocktails. It was a procedure that took more than 15 minutes to correctly complete according to the family recipe. Unlike many of their surrounding neighbors in the burgeoning bar business, Ramos heeded the 18th Amendment and closed the Imperial Cabinet Saloon when alcohol consumption was declared illegal.

After Prohibition, Henry spilled the secret and sold the rights to his name and the gin fizz recipe to the Roosevelt Hotel. The drink's popularity survived and grew, largely due to men like Huey Long and places such as the Roosevelt.

Above: Henry C. Ramos
Left: The Ramos Gin Fizz was invented in 1888 by Ramos at his bar in the Meyer's Restauraunt on the corner of Carondelet and Gravier Streets in the Central Business District.

"I'm sampling these to make certain you gentlemen are getting the real thing."

Huey Long

In response to reporters at the Roosevelt Hotel in New York City after consuming five Ramos Gin Fizzes

None may be as dedicated to a single cocktail as Louisiana's past governor and senator, Huey Long. He was most fond of the Ramos Gin Fizz, and he was most fond of drinking them inside of the Roosevelt Hotel, now known as The Fairmont.

Long's love of the cocktail was intense, and his flamboyant antics when intoxicated garnered him unflattering front-page coverage, often for weeks at a time. With his reputation headed for dire straits, he decided to sober up.

The story unfolds that in 1935, while preparing for the presidential election in '36, Long took a business trip to New York, and it didn't take long for the lure of one particular libation to crush his self-imposed sobriety.

Convinced that no citizen of New York could possibly get a decent Ramos Gin Fizz, Huey Long insisted on flying bartender Sam Guarino from the Roosevelt Hotel in New Orleans to the sister hotel in New York. Arriving in the Big Apple, Guarino was beseeched by Long to train the northern staff on the proper Big Easy mixology for the cocktail. Long began to taste test, consuming not one but five.

There are other tales that claim Huey Long actually built Highway 61 with the sole intention of a faster trip from the Capitol building in Baton Rouge. The highway runs directly to the Roosevelt and his beloved drink.

Ramos Gin Fizz

Cracked ice
2 oz. gin
3 dashes orange flower water
1 oz. lemon juice
1/4 oz. lime juice
1 egg white
1 oz. cream (or half-and-half)
1 tsp. sugar
Soda water

Pour all ingredients over cracked ice in a shaker. Shake vigorously for at least one minute. Strain into a chilled tumbler and top with soda water.

***Left**: Huey Long's famous tutorial on making a proper Ramos Gin Fizz captured here in 1935 at the Roosevelt Hotel in New York City.*

Contrary to the notion that Bourbon Street is named for its plethora of merry-makers roused and reveling by the amber liquid, it actually earned the nomen in the same manner of almost all of the other French Quarter streets. Streets in the Vieux Carre were named after royal houses in France, and Bourbon is no exception. Its name is a tribute to the House of Bourbon, which was the ruling dynasty in France when the city of New Orleans was built.

A drunk man in evening clothes and top hat leaning against a Bourbon Street sign was at one time a popular souvenir sold in the French Quarter. The example pictured at right is cast iron and hand painted, circa 1950.

II

LEGENDARY LOCATIONS

Serving for hundreds of years, the oldest bars and restaurants of New Orleans are saturated in legends. Alcohol has tempted and twisted the retelling of these histories, and truth is often mixed with myth and a heavy-handed pour.

ANTOINE'S
ANTOINE'S RESTAURANT
ANTOINE'S RESTAURANT.

ANTOINE'S

Antoine Alciatore

A place gilded in the wealth and abundance of the New World, New Orleans to Antoine Alciatore was an untapped culinary oasis. He viewed his market as the city's most affluent, and when he opened his small *pension* in 1840, at the tender age of 27, he leaned on his French heritage and cooking skills acquired during his childhood in France. His penchant for decadence intoxicated New Orleans' wealthy, and Pension Alciatore garnered a loyalty in the first five years that exceeded the means of the humble space.

Antoine, with the help of his new wife and sister-in-law, moved the family business down the street to its current-day residence at 713 St. Louis in 1868. The *pension* was becoming more of a restaurant than boarding house, and the family traditions that would span five generations into the future were merely beginning.

In 1874, Antoine foresaw his own passing, and wishing to die in his native country, he handed the responsibilities to his son Jules. Jules carried the restaurant into the next century on pride and the invention of dishes such as Oysters Rockefeller. Named after the richest man in the world at that time and for its own decadence, Oysters Rockefeller was just one of the immense contributions Jules Alciatore made towards establishing his native city as a culinary capital of the world. The true recipe for Oysters Rockefeller has remained a family secret that multitudes have attempted to imitate since.

During Prohibition, the Alciatore family upheld a façade in keeping with the high society they served, and gracious adherence to the law was practiced in the dining rooms. When a gentleman felt the need for a nip of brandy, however, he might retire to the Ladies Room, where once inside, he would find a secret passage to a bartender, standing in a room outfitted with a sawdust floor. The bartender would stipulate a vow of secrecy and fill a coffee cup with the desired contraband. If the customer was asked what he was drinking upon returning to the table, he would gently reply, "It's a mystery."

Hence, the room became The Mystery Room when it was utilized formally post-Prohibition.

Antoine's is where America comes to dine. This statement is not a slogan. It is fact, just as it is a fact that it is the oldest restaurant in America still owned and operated by the same family.

The classic occurrence of New Orleans-born waiters who can recall decades on the job is commonplace, and the walls are lined with thousands of autographed pictures of celebrities, politicians, sports figures and icons of business. Lisa Marie Presley has dined at the same table as her father Elvis Presley before her, both served by the same waiter. This is legendary yet routine inside of the 15 dining rooms that comprise the building today. It is just one among hundreds of stories lining the annals of Antoine's.

Above: The current menu cover design used in the dining rooms today was created in 1940. It debuted at the 100th birthday celebration, and the cover has remained exactly the same ever since.

Right: This drawing could be found on the cover of the menu at Antoine's during the years between 1910 and 1940.

There is no actual bar inside of the 15 dining rooms that make up Antoine's restaurant. It is a firm belief of the family that drink only goes with food, and the two shall not be separated inside of the building. But lighting either food or drink on fire is absolutely accepted.

Café Brulôt Diabolique

In the late 1800s, Jules Alciatore created Antoine's signature Café Brulôt Diabolique. It was a twist on a French ceremony of years past in which bon vivants would soak a sugar cube in Cognac and place it over an open flame before dipping it in coffee.

His Café Brulôt Diabolique was a grander display, and it is a combination of the three things that make an evening at Antoine's spectacular — the wafting of smell, the heaven of taste and the luxury of opulent ambiance. Served at the end of a meal, the lights are dimmed and shadows cast as a snake of blue flame is seemingly conjured from the bowl and bent to the will of the waiter.

The serving cups, which display a crimson devil, and the copper Brulot bowls were commissioned by Jules Alciatore.

3 oz. brandy
3 cups strong black coffee, hot
2 cinnamon sticks
8 whole cloves
1 whole lemon peel
1-½ tbsp. sugar

Combine cinnamon, cloves, lemon peel, sugar and brandy in a fireproof bowl and heat on an open flame. When the brandy is hot, but not boiling, bring the bowl to the table and ignite with a match. Stir and pour the mixture around the bowl for 2 minutes. Pour the coffee into the flaming brandy to extinguish the flames. Ladle into demitasse cups.

ARNAUD
813

ARNAUD'S

Named for the signature cocktail of Cognac and Champagne, the French 75 Bar in Arnaud's restaurant complements the cocktail's decadent taste with 1920s French-influenced decor and ambiance.

As colorful as any character in the history of New Orleans, Count Arnaud Cazenave was actually not born of royal bloodlines. The nickname "Count" was given to him by his friends, and he had no issues with adopting it. The name was justified, however, since Count Arnaud would secure his place in history as a monarch of the culinary trade.

Cazenave was working as a wine salesman in the city when he opened his restaurant Arnaud's in 1918. Somewhat of a champion for the finer things in life, he had high opinions of the importance of food and beverage on everyday life, and he expressed his beliefs in public and on the back of each menu as his "Philosophy of Dining."

He wrote, "A dinner chosen according to one's needs, tastes and moods, well prepared and well served, is a joy to all senses and an impelling incentive to sound sleep, good health and long life. Therefore, at least once a day, preferably in the quiet cool of the evening, one should throw all care to the winds, relax completely and dine leisurely and well."

As the city grew, locals adopted his philosophy, and Arnaud's became one of the top restaurants in the country during the 1930s and 1940s. Cazenave secured property with the same vigor that he secured patronage, and the physical walls of his restaurant were under constant expansion. Today, Arnaud's comprises 13 buildings, among them a few converted brothels and opium dens, and the kitchen is the largest freestanding kitchen in New Orleans.

Opening the year before Prohibition presented obstacles. The telltale coffee cups could be found in Arnaud's just as they could in every other establishment, and the back garbage-alley door became a common portico for those in need of port or brandy. Count Arnaud reportedly filled his own cup each morning with his version of "half-and-half" — half coffee, half bourbon — consuming multiple cups in a day. The Count's own indulgence did not go unnoticed. He was imprisoned for a short time but was later exonerated after an eloquent speech in which he convinced a jury of the necessity of serving alcohol with food.

When the Count passed away in 1948, his flamboyant daughter Germaine Cazenave Wells stepped into the dining room spotlight. Known for her fascination with anything alcoholic, it was Germaine who bolstered the lively atmosphere in the already-established Richelieu bar and added to it by opening another lounge that is now known as the French 75 Bar.

Germaine didn't march to the beat of a different drummer — she danced. She often found mirth in mandating what entire tables would drink with dinner, once going so far as to demand that one table consume nothing but Tequila Sunrises. Germaine also is credited with starting the Easter Bonnet Parade, now renamed the Historic French Quarter Parade.

French 75

Germaine Cazenave Wells was fond of a Scarlett O'Hara, but she was an even greater devotee of the French 75 cocktail. Current owner of Arnaud's, Archie Casbarian, named the largest bar in the restaurant after her favorite cocktail in 1978, and the drink has become a signature at the venue.

The cocktail is named for the French 75 cannon used during the First World War, and its creation myth also includes the allegation that American Army officers supposedly drank it from the castings of 75-millimeter shells.

Its original recipe is a source of contention. Some claim gin, others pour Cognac. At Arnaud's, naturally, the recipe calls for the French variation.

1 ½ oz. Cognac
1 tsp. fresh lemon juice
¼ tsp. simple syrup
Champagne as needed, about 4 oz.
Twist of lemon

Place Cognac, lemon juice and simple syup in a shaker filled with ice and shake only long enough to chill. Pour into a frosted Champagne glass, top with Champagne and add a lemon twist. Serve immediately.

One of New Orleans most famous characters, Count Arnaud Cazenave stands in front of his mansion at 544 Esplanade Avenue that is said he still haunts. The Count believed that fine living was dependant upon refined food and elegant drinks, and his French 75 cocktail, combining premium Champagne and French Cognac, was a proud testament to the theory.

BRENNAN'S

Known in his lifetime as "The Happy Irishman of the French Quarter," Owen Edward Brennan's ancestry may have been true Irish, but his soul was New Orleans, his charm contagious. Never one to shy from hard work and deep devotion, Brennan supported himself, his extensive family and the city in more ways than mere reliance on time and money would ever have allowed.

In 1943, Prohibition was over and The Old Absinthe House was where people came to drink in Owen Brennan's flair for ambiance. It was there that he began to build an empire based on shaking hands once and remembering names forever. It would be the cornerstone ideal that still honors the Brennan's family name these many decades hence.

Brennan's Restaurant, probably following some of its own Irish heritage, was born of a bet. Count Arnaud taunted Owen that a restaurant was too much for an Irish-born drinker to accomplish. In 1946, Owen Brennan signed the lease on the space across from his Old Absinthe House and christened it Owen Brennan's French & Creole Restaurant. The populace at large would later shorten it to Owen Brennan's Vieux Carré.

As Brennan's venue name grew shorter and shorter until ultimately becoming simply Brennan's, Owen Brennan's name grew larger and more elaborate with time. Called both "The Wonder Man," and "a one man Chamber of Commerce," Owen Edward Brennan was one of America's first great establishers of the brand. In his most famous competitive moment, he went after the profits of the neighboring restaurant Antoine's. When Francis Parkinson Keyes published *Dinner at Antoine's*, Brennan strode forth with his call of "Breakfast at Brennan's." He took the most important meal of the day and made it a social event spanning three to four hours. As important as being seen in church on Sunday, New Orleanians lined the walkway to attend brunch at Brennan's. The hair of the dog that bit you was redesigned there, elevated and refined, in cocktails like the Bloody Mary, Brennan's own Brandy Milk Punch and the Mimosa. Brennan called these his "eye openers," and while there is no full proof, he is often credited with inventing that category name. Whether it's myth or fact, he is definitely responsible for making it an American turn of phrase.

Today, Brennan's still serves hundreds of Mimosas a morning, still employs the old-world-service idea of Captains, still offers the original dish of Grillades and Grits and still has a hand on the pulse of everything that matters in service. There are men working in the kitchen who can enlighten visitors about days when Martinis on the patio cost a nickel, a crazy Sunday when the staff served 1,700 people before 2 p.m. and the day that Mr. Brennan hired them to wash dishes but trained them to be chefs.

Mimosa

3 oz. Champagne, chilled
3 oz. orange juice, chilled
1 whole strawberry
1 orange slice

Pour Champagne into a chilled stemmed glass, then add orange juice. Stir gently. Drop strawberry into glass and garnish with orange slice.

Before he was known for Brennan's Restaurant, Owen Brennan owned The Old Absinthe House. It was there that he began to build an empire based on shaking hands once and remembering names forever.

CAROUSEL BAR

New Orleans is a city where every bar claims to be a cultural attaché and every barkeep the man who has seen it all. Each nook and cranny is stuffed to the zydeco-drenched rafters with tall tales about the legends of both the stage and page. In this city, the average Joe can easily find himself atop a barstool taking shots with them. From the velvet throats that graced the vinyl of Americana, to the authors who have touched generations with their tales, New Orleans' watering holes are home to all.

Born from the old Swan Room, where Liberace was the first ticket on the bill, the Carousel Piano Bar and Lounge has sat all but motionless inside the Hotel Monteleone for 56 years. The carousel itself stands as an elegantly carved witness to American history — a physical symbol of New Orleans' sense of revelry. Beneath the slow revolving sparkle of eight jesters on the outer rim and eight cherubs underneath there are both sin and merriment here, tall tales and truth.

Authors and musicians flocked to the Carousel because they could mingle with regular society and reconnect with the atmosphere that is at the true heart of the French Quarter. Tennessee Williams and Truman Capote once hid in the high-backed booths to eavesdrop on stories of the lechery and exploits of New Orleans society. Musicians from Etta James to Gregg Allman have sat on the slow revolving painted wooden barstools or touched the keys of the adjoining piano.

While the space is actually two rooms, with the carousel in one and the piano in other, it's the revolving bar itself that beckons visitors in off Royal Street and draws them to the Hotel Monteleone from around the globe. It is a spiritual experience, both in glasses and ghosts. An afternoon spent sipping a Brandy Alexander on the same stool where Tennessee Williams did the same years ago, as the foot traffic of Royal Street is displayed like a stage play through the bay windows — that is the romance and the alluring appeal of The Carousel Piano Bar and Lounge.

New Orleans' first revolving bar, shown here, was installed in the Hotel Monteleone in 1949.

Vieux Carré Cocktail

Named after the original French name for the Old Quarter, the Vieux Carré cocktail was developed by Walter Bergeron in 1938 when he was working as the head bartender at the Hotel Monteleone. The drink has been tied to this French Quarter institution ever since.

Ice cubes
1/8 tsp. Benedictine
2 dashes Peychaud's Bitters®
2 dashes Angostura Bitters®
3/4 oz. each of rye whiskey, Cognac, Italian vermouth

Combine all ingredients in a rocks glass over ice. Stir and garnish with a lemon twist.

In 1992, the carousel's facade was updated. The jester carvings and mirrors adorn the outside canopy, with eight cherub carvings surrounding the inner rim. The Carousel Bar is a miniature version of a larger Dentzel carousel in California.

"In this profession it's a long walk between drinks."

Truman Capote

Born in New Orleans in 1924 to a 16-year-old beauty queen named Lillie Mae Faulk, Truman Capote was not, as both he and some of the hotel staff liked to claim, born in the lobby of the Hotel Monteleone. His mother did spend the last few days of her pregnancy in a suite at the hotel, but Truman was born in Uptown at the Touro Infimary.

Capote's works were heavily influenced by his native city. Although he preferred to think of home as the Big Apple instead of the Big Easy, his flamboyant manner and wanderlust for the next great cocktail party were instinctively and intrinsically New Orleans.

When declared frivolous, he claimed he was working on a book. When asked his cocktail of preference, he claimed "my orange drink." Truman Capote was the consummate fan of the Screwdriver.

Screwdriver

Ice cubes
2 oz. vodka
5 oz. fresh orange juice
Orange slice

Pour vodka and orange juice into a glass filled with ice cubes. Stir gently and garnish with orange slice.

***Left:** Photographed here by Carl Van Vechten in 1948, Truman Capote earned an O. Henry Award that year for his work "Shut a Final Door."*

COLUMNS HOTEL

A guest of The Columns Hotel once wrote, "I came to New Orleans to discover New Orleans, and I found her at The Columns." The structure's history mimics the city's own. A grand old dame, she has seen both buggies and Bentleys pass on St. Charles Avenue. Under her eaves rest tales of both triumph and tenacity — followed and preceded by sordid sadness and ill repute.

Built by the city's architect du jour Thomas Sully in the late 1880s, the building was originally designed as a private residence commissioned by Simon Hernsheim. As owner and operator of the large tobacco company Hernsheim Brothers & Co., he made regular voyages to Havana for cigars, often returning with extra cargo of mahogany for his stately home. Today, The Columns Hotel has more original mahogany wood than any other in the city.

Hernsheim was a haunted man and after the death of his wife he took his own life in his factory in 1898. In 1915, the structure became a private boarding house. It remained quite exclusive during that time, but when it was restructured as a hotel in the 1940s, deterioration began to creep inward from the corners. Ceilings were dropped for economic reasons, and columns were encased and hidden from the world.

Most famous for its role as the set in Louis Malle's 1978 movie "Pretty Baby" starring Brooke Shields, the house at that time rented rooms for as little as $10 a night. It was never a bordello, but, as the movie set, it offered a glimpse into the lives of prostitutes and photographer E. J. Bellocq in the early 1900s.

Ernest J. Bellocq was one of the only photographers to ever capture the city's red-light district in its harsh, naked reality. The district was called Storyville for the district's alderman, Sidney Story. The bordellos of Storyville were shut down when prostitution was declared illegal in 1917, but prostitutes, like alcohol during Prohibition, were still inseparable from the city of New Orleans.

It is not known if E. J. Bellocq ever visited the boarding house on St. Charles, but some of his original photographs of New Orleans' "working girls" hang in the attic rooms now known as the Bellocq and Pretty Baby suites.

Currently, the Columns Hotel is owned and operated by Jacques and Claire Creppel, who purchased and restored it in 1980. The Victorian Lounge is now one of the country's most illustrious bars. Outfitted with the trappings of yesteryear, there is a foot press for service in the floor, leftover from the room's original use as a dining parlor. The home's original chandelier was refurbished out of fragments that spent decades in the attic, and it once again casts light on new traditions and classic cocktails alike.

Right: Raleigh Rye was the drink of choice in most brothels and bordellos in Storyville. One of E. J. Bellocq's most famous photos pictures a prostitute sitting in striped stockings with a bottle of Raleigh Rye on the table, a glass in her hand and a faraway look in her eye.

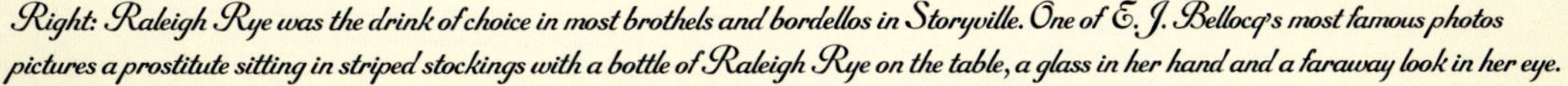

Current owners Jacques and Claire Creppel restored the Columns Hotel to its former glamour in the 1980s. The Victorian Lounge was once the main dining room of the house, and the mantelpiece and overmantel in this room are the only remaining examples of this kind of design by famous New Orleans architect Thomas Sully.

This photo, taken by E. J. Bellocq around 1912, depicts two Storyville "workers" passing the time playing cards.

Pretty Baby

The recipe for the Pretty Baby cocktail was written by Columns Hotel bartender Mike Smith and current owner Claire Creppel around 1983. The drink was mixed for the first time as a 17-year-old Brooke Shields watched. According the Claire Creppel, she was still too young to drink it, so the drink was meant to honor her persona rather than appealing to her personal preferences. It was mixed to be pretty and elegant, but not too terribly sweet. Shields and her namesake cocktail can be found in the Victorian Lounge quite often, and she admits that the movie and the house were her inspiration for her thesis at Princeton.

The only known likeness of E. J. Bellocq.

Ice cubes
2 oz. vodka
2 oz. white créme de cacao
2 oz. milk
Splash of grenadine
Maraschino cherry
Nutmeg

Combine vodka, white créme de cacao and milk over ice in a shaker and shake. Strain into a tall glass filled with ice. Add a splash of grenadine and stir. Garnish with a sprinkle of nutmeg and maraschino cherry and serve with a straw.

Galatoire's

Since 1905

GALATOIRE'S

Whether ordering a house Martini, served "unadulterated," on the rocks with no vermouth, or a Galatoire's Special Cocktail, a Sazerac served with bourbon instead of the usual rye whiskey, every guest at Galatoire's can be guaranteed one thing — the glass will always be refilled before the ice even contemplates contact with the bottom of the tumbler.

A tradition built on three-hour lunches followed directly by three-hour dinners, Galatoire's is home away from home when marking a special event. For five generations, the Galatoire family has run a business built on honoring each customer's celebrations in life, or simply honoring each weekend's arrival. Lines stretch down the sidewalk as early as 8:30 a.m. on regular Fridays, and with the weekend mere hours away, many make lunch an excuse to exonerate the rest of the workday and remain until dinner. Ceiling fans with tiny bulbs arc in lazy circles above a scene that blurs the lines between sit-down meal and all-out cocktail party. People migrate from table to table, their cocktails magically appearing refreshed and ready at each table they choose to visit, and the waiters double as decision makers when most request "whatever looks good today."

Jean Galatoire began the traditions enjoyed today when he opened Galatoire's on Bourbon in 1905. Brought from Pardies, France, the recipes were passed down for generations before him, and harmonious in simplicity, they have endured ever since. Little of the original has changed inside the sainted space. The no-reservations policy for the downstairs dining room is legendary and immune to the evolution of the outside world.

The Friday lunch before Christmas and the Friday lunch before Mardi Gras are singular events at Galatoire's. The no-reservations policy remains on these prestigious days, but in recent years patrons began queuing up, or paying someone to stand in line, earlier and earlier. Eventually, people were patiently waiting — and living — outside Galatoire's a full three days ahead of Friday Mardi Gras lunch.

For these occasions, a reception is now held on the preceding Monday. One-hundred and fifty paddles are awarded on a first come, first serve basis, and the 24 tables are sold at auction, with the money donated to local charities. The Monday before Mardi Gras in 2007, an astounding $100,000 was collected from those loyal patrons who could not bear to eat Friday lunch anywhere else. Restaurants simply don't build a reputation like this any more — not like Galatoire's.

Ojen Cocktail

The anise liqueur Ojen (pronounced ohen) is named for the town of Ojen, Spain where it was produced for hundreds of years. As was the custom, Spanish men were once inclined to drink Ojen early in the morning with their coffee. Another tradition, according to the Krewe of Rex, is that drinking an Ojen cocktail before marching on Mardi Gras day brings good luck. Unfortunately, the Emanuel Fernandez Distillery, the only maker of Ojen, has discontinued the production of the liqueur. Although, it is rumored that Martin's Wine Cellar in New Orleans has stockpiled all of the Ojen available, making it possible for the Krewe of Rex to keep toasting on "Fat Tuesday" and for Galatoire's restaurant to keep serving its famous Ojen cocktail.

Crushed ice
3 oz. Ojen liqueur
2 dashes of Peychaud's Bitters®

Fill rocks glass with crushed ice. Pour liqueur over ice. Add dashes of Peychaud's Bitters on top and allow it to permeate the drink before serving.

Right: Galatoire's legendary downstairs dining room.

Brandy Alexander

Williams was quoted once that he needed a good drink after a long day of writing when he was completely "spent with the rigors of creation." He was a regular fixture at many a cocktail joint around town including the Hotel Monteleone, Galatoire's, the New Orleans Athletic Club and Antoine's. For legends unknown, the Brandy Alexander is the cocktail immediately associated with this literary French Quarter regular. It was probably not his true favorite, but he was a boost for that cocktail's reputation. It has been riding the coattails of his ghost for decades.

1 ¼ oz. brandy
¾ oz. dark crème de cacao
4 oz. half-and-half
Nutmeg

Combine all ingredients along with ice in a cocktail shaker and shake well until frothy and chilled. Strain into a martini glass and sprinkle with fresh nutmeg.

The letter shown at left was written by Tennessee Williams in 1947 to Pancho Rodriguez, complaining about the high New York City rents and asking how Pancho fared in the recent New Orleans hurricane.

"Life is as much a merry tavern as a sad hotel." *Tennessee Williams*

Thomas Lanier Williams' grandfather was an Episcopal minister named Walter Dankin, and the Reverend Dankin brought a very young Thomas to the Hotel Monteleone for his first tastes of New Orleans. It is said that on one of those visits, when Reverend Dankin went to pay the bill as they were leaving, the man at the desk replied, "You have been the guest of Mr. Monteleone. There will be no charge."

The young Thomas, apparently, never lost sight of how that one moment made him feel important. His love for the city of New Orleans inspired him to permanently adopt his more colorful college nickname when he moved to the French Quarter in 1939.

He became known to the world as Tennessee Williams.

His works of fiction were streaked with real-life events from his past and his lifelong affection for the city of New Orleans. A man-about-town, Williams had a table at Galatoire's, a barstool at Dixie's Bar of Music, a midnight passion for "Miss Lily" Hood's piano playing at Lafitte's, and a tendency to hide out at the Napoleon House during the slower, afternoon hours.

Tennessee Williams met Pancho Rodriguez while traveling in Mexico. The two became lovers and were living together during the days when Williams was working on "A Streetcar Named Desire." Still friends years later, the two were photographed at Pat O' Briens.

Rue Bourbon
Bourbon
St. Philip
Lafitte's
Blacksmith Shop

LAFITTE'S BLACKSMITH SHOP

In the early 1800's, pirate brothers Jean and Pierre Lafitte found a refuge from the high seas in the bayous south of New Orleans. In 1809, Louisiana was a newly acquired portion of America, and the unscrupulous pair opened a shop on the corner of Bourbon and St. Peter under the front of blacksmithing. While it is believed that nary a horse was shod there, liquor and ill-gotten plunder were in heavy supply. Slaves could even be purchased at Lafitte's Blacksmith Shop for a price that was far lower than the contemporary going rate.

The law overlooked Lafitte's for the most part, but on one occasion, Governor William Claiborne posted a number of handbills offering $500 for Jean Lafitte's capture. Lafitte returned the gesture with advertisements offering $5,000 for the governor's head.

Claiborne and Jean Lafitte reconciled their differences when British ships began to crest the horizon. In a show of rare honesty, the pirate became a privateer, fighting the Battle of New Orleans alongside Andrew Jackson. The battle concluded with more than 2,000 dead on the British side to Jackson and Lafitte's six casualties. Jackson would later offer a pardon to Lafitte when he took office as President of the United States.

Argued to be one of the nation's oldest bars, Lafitte's Blacksmith Shop is one of the only remaining French architectural structures left from before the fires of 1788 and 1794. The popular style of architecture during this colonial period was known as brick-between-posts. Large missing chunks of plaster in Lafitte's bar display this construction method that was no longer utilized in the post-fire structures.

On both the inside and outside of the structure on the corner of Bourbon and St. Peter Streets there are large chunks of plaster missing. You can see the brick-between-posts method of construction from the colonial period.

The only electric lights are behind the bar, and the remaining illumination is by candle. Amidst the rickety wooden tables, candles and firelight provide bouncing shadows to accompany the piano player in the corner, and exposed brick and beam give the place its charm. Lafitte's has known a multitude of owners in its two-and-a-quarter centuries. In the 1950s, owner Tom Caplinger was particularly generous, giving away free drinks to friends like Tennessee Williams, and he left a legacy of extensive debt.

Left: Sometime before Hurricane Katrina hit, this framed portrait of Jean Lafitte mysteriously disappeared from its place on a wall inside the bar.

Pirate's Punch

Ice
1 ½ oz. dark rum
¾ oz. light rum
½ oz. 151-proof rum
1 ½ oz. fresh pineapple juice
½ oz. fresh orange juice
¼ oz. fresh lime juice
¼ oz. grenadine
Orange slice
Maraschino cherry

Pour all ingredients except for orange slice and Maraschino cherry into a cocktail shaker. Shake until mixed and well chilled. Pour into a tall, chilled cocktail glass with ice. Garnish with orange slice and Maraschino cherry

400.00

NAPOLEON HOUSE

Even the dirt inside is charming, and everything is coated in gentle layers of that charm. The lightbulbs seem destined to dim at any moment. Clad in bowties — a few sporting full mustaches and long sideburns — the waiters pouring out the bar's signature Pimm's Cups appear to be leftovers from a time when the walls wore fresh paint.

The oldest part of the structure at 500 Rue Chartres was built by Claude François Girod in 1797, but the section now known as the Napoleon House was completed by his brother, Mayor Nicholas Girod, in 1814. In 1821, Nicholas Girod offered the building to Napoleon in his exile — as a refuge and a symbol of the friendship and hospitality New Orleans sought to offer. Jean Lafitte was empowered to send a ship, *La Séraphine*, to carry Napoleon to his new home in Louisiana, but three days before the tides would take the *Séraphine*, Napoleon went home to meet his maker.

This story is recounted as every carriage driver urges the horse to pull round the Chartres Street corner; every visitor is sent home with a scrap of history no one can prove. There is no proof that the alleged ship meant to sail, or that the ship herself even existed. That matters little to the bar. It inspires the retelling and has born the name and the liquor license since the mid 1900s.

While the Napoleon House changed hands multiple times in the late 1800s, Joseph Impastato rented the building in 1914 for $20 a month and ran it as a grocery downstairs with living quarters for his family above. The Impastato family purchased the building in 1920 for a price tag of $14,000, and Joe lived there past his 100th birthday, passing the business down to his brother Peter during World War II.

NAPOLEON HOUSE, NEW ORLEANS, LA.

Salvatore Impastato took over in 1971 and has changed almost nothing. The scarred walls host portraits of past family members, odd paintings that were either sold to Peter Impastato by struggling artists or rented out in exchange for cash in hand. Knowing exactly how something made its way onto the picked and peeling walls of the Napoleon House is about as easy as predicting the date it will come down. In a show of his tenacity for letting history determine décor, when one of the pictures warped and fell from its frame, Salvatore just left the empty frame on the wall. From the classical music played off of albums to the register behind the bar sitting silent and broken under a clay bust of Napoleon, the atmosphere and ambiance have little truck with modern time. The register was once set to read $18.03 as the final sale, alluding to the date that marks the Louisiana Purchase, but a short circuit sent the numbers sliding to $400.00. In typical fashion, no one has lifted a finger to fix it.

Pimm's Cup

The Pimm's Cup has become as synonymous with The Napoleon House over the years as the story of Napoleon's wasted rescue plans. The irony of a British tonic supporting the profits of a decidedly French-loving bar is overlooked and buried under the fine layers of sunset-tinted dust and idle, afternoon conversations.

Ice cubes
1½-1¾ oz. *Pimm's No.1®*
7-Up,®
Cucumber Slice

Fill a tall Collins glass with ice cubes. Add 7-Up till three-fourth's full. Add Pimm's to fill. Stir well and garnish with cucumber slice.

A sunrise view of the French Quarter rooftops and cupola of the Napoleon House.

The New Orleans Athletic Club claims to have wet the brows of Clarke Gable and "Tarzan" star Johnny Weissmuller with a challenging workout in the gym and indoor pool. Whether the pair then wet their whistles in the adjoining bar is not known. Photographed here, the bar hosts liquor bottles and old trophies in almost equal numbers.

NEW ORLEANS ATHLETIC CLUB

In every other part of the world, drinking and exercising are opposing events. New Orleans is not like any other part of the world, and in typical *bon vivant* style, at the New Orleans Athletic Club on North Rampart, you can drink a Mimosa after a morning on the Stairmaster.

The club originated in 1872 in a Faubourg area warehouse, and the sign outside read, "Young Men's Gymnastic Club." In 1890, it moved to its present French Quarter location and became the New Orleans Athletic Club. The building was erected in 1929, and sweat, blood and spirits could all be found within.

The actual bar inside the building was a man's domain, with legendary fighters like Pete Herman and John Sullivan drinking after long training sessions in the same room that now displays their likenesses in photos on the wall. The bar at one time was open 24 hours a day, 364 and 1/2 days a year. When the Christmas bells chimed at 12:01 a.m. on Christmas morning, the doors were locked — only to open again at 12:01 p.m. on the same day for business.

Legendary boxer John L. Sullivan trained in the New Orleans Athletic Club for his seventy-four-round bare-knuckled 1889 fight with Jake Kilrain.

It is said of the NOAC that there was a time in the city's history where you couldn't be mayor without first being a member there. Every blue blood in the city had a connection to the club, and every aspiring businessman sidled up next to them at the bar with grand aspirations of future fortune.

NOAC's golden years reigned from the 1920s to the 1960s. Its popularity faltered slightly in the 1970s, but a man named Ed Vaughan refused to lose his favorite place to drink. In the mid '70s, Vaughan was in his 70s, and it is said that he would consume a six-pack of Budweiser every day at the club before returning to his French Quarter apartment in a taxi. Such was his love for the place, that he bailed it out financially with new barstools and fresh paint. In his honor, the bar is now known as Vaughan's Pub.

Rumor has it that one well-known local has developed his own "executive workout." It begins with a long stroll through the club, several hellos and brief conversations, a short steam and then a seat at the end of the long copper-topped bar. He then asks for a "health drink." Fresh squeezed orange juice is added to his vodka, and calling it a screwdriver is totally out of the question.

"Civilization begins with distillation."

William Faulkner

When William Faulkner moved to New Orleans from his home in Oxford, Mississippi in 1925, it is reported that he strode into town to meet his mentor, author Sherwood Anderson, wearing a coat lined with hidden pockets. In those pockets, Faulkner had stashed bottles of Mississippi moonshine, fearing that he wouldn't be able to find a drink in the city. Amongst the torrid temperatures and local characters, he made his home at 624 Pirate's Alley, and in those Prohibition-gripped days he produced his first novel, *Soldiers' Pay*, his second work *Mosquitoes* and a great deal of bathtub gin. He shortly returned to Oxford, and while many of his works are penned in the vernacular of northern Mississippi, it can't be denied that Faulkner took more than a sentence and sip from dear old New Orleans.

Marvin's Mint Julep a la Creole

This recipe is courtesy of Hotel Monteleone's Carousel Piano Bar & Lounge veteran bartender, Marvin Allen. This recipe is a great example of an innovative twist on an old New Orleans classic.

Crushed ice
1 ½ oz. Old New Orleans Rum®
6 to 8 fresh mint leaves
2 ripe, fresh strawberries
1 to 2 cane sugar cubes depending on the sweetness of the strawberry
Sprig of mint

Muddle mint leaves, one strawberry and sugar cubes in the bottom of a Julep cup with enough water to melt the sugar. Fill cup with crushed ice and pour in rum. Garnish with mint sprig and remaining strawberry.

Left: Carl Van Vechten photograph of William Faulkner in 1954.

The Old Absinthe House walls are covered in faded business cards and signed scraps of paper from past patrons. This tradition was said to have been started by Owen Brennan sometime after he purchased the establishment in 1943.

OLD ABSINTHE HOUSE

Constructed in 1806 by Pedro Front and Francisco Juncadelia of Barcelona, the building on the corner of Bienville and Bourbon has so much history in its walls that if they began to talk the whole Quarter would hush to hear the stories. Originally, it housed an importing and commission firm, but in 1846 the lower-floor front room was established as Aleix's Coffee House — operated by Jacinto Aleix and his brother, the nephews of Señor Juncadelia. The building's illustrious history would truly begin when resident mixologist Cayetano Ferrer made the very first Absinthe Frappe there. "The Absinthe Room" was born in 1874.

Absinthe — the word hisses on the befitting middle syllable, like a proclamation of promised taboo. Its guile and green hue enticed the artists, the poets, the poverty-stricken and the highly esteemed. So branding a bar as the official and local promoter of the liquid was bound to lend the trappings of legends.

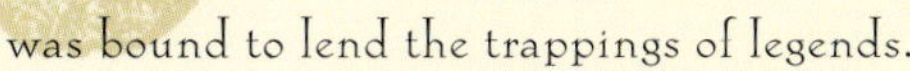

Oscar Wilde and Mark Twain. P.T. Barnum and Theodore Roosevelt. The building knew the personal conversations of each throughout history, but perhaps the most famous conversation was between New Orleans' personal Pirate Jean Lafitte and Andrew Jackson. The building is said to have housed a secret floor, one where Lafitte and Jackson discussed their plans for The Battle of New Orleans long into the night. The room is since found, the conversation's specifics long lost, and all of it may be more of an apocryphal addition to The Absinthe's lore than any kind of truth.

When absinthe was declared illegal in 1912, an outcry went up. The sign stayed on the front of the building at that point known as "The Old Absinthe House," and inside, the silver absinthe spoons were kept moist. Single drops of water still fell on each sugar cube, dissolving into the murky green liquid beneath — only now it was slightly less out in the open. The Old Absinthe House not only continued to serve illegal liquor, it served the most illegal of them all. In great defiance, the bar served absinthe some 20 years past the ban.

A sculpture of Napoleon adorns the top of this green marble absinthe fountain.

DANCING
JAX
BEER
BOURBON ST.
ONE WAY STREET
The Old Absinthe House

Photographed here in 1954 by C. F. Webber, The Old Absinthe House's "secret floor" fan transoms are visible at the tops of the first floor doorways.

Unfortunately for the artists and other nonconformist regulars, authorities caught wind and raided the building shortly after Prohibition began. Anonymous friends of the bar smuggled out the four remaining items that weren't destroyed by the police. This included the original pitted bar, the clock and two original absinthe fountains. The items were moved to a warehouse on Bourbon, which subsequently simply opened under the name, "The Old Absinthe Bar." The green liquid and New Orleans were meant to reunite at all costs, it seems.

Today, the original bar is located back in its birthplace, which now offers drinkers a choice of Italian food in the adjoining Tony Moran's Restaurant. Big wrought-iron chandeliers cast soft light on the hundreds of faded business cards adorning the walls. A tradition begun by Owen Brennan when he owned the space in the mid 1900s, the effect is like sitting inside of a scrapbook. Aleister Crowley wrote his work "Absinthe — The Green Goddess" inside The Old Absinthe House while waiting on a friend, and his words seem as true today as they did when he penned them in 1918. "Art is the soul of life, and the Old Absinthe House is the heart and soul of the old quarter of New Orleans."

One of the most discussed segments of The Old Absinthe House has always been the «entresol» or hidden floor. It was this room where Jean Lafitte and Andrew Jackson supposedly planned the Battle of New Orleans. The entresol also had a more current employment as the set for the private detective offices in the TV series "Bourbon Street Beat" which aired from 1959 to 1960.

Silver-screen stars Joseph Cotten and Teresa Wright were photographed inspecting the Old Absinthe House plaque while on location for the filming of "The Steel Trap" in 1952. The two had also starred together in Alfred Hitchcock's "Shadow of a Doubt" released nine years earlier in 1943.

Have
Fun

PAT O'BRIEN'S

A lot goes into the making of a Hurricane cocktail — a lot of liquor and a lot of history. Benson Harrison "Pat" O'Brien is credited with creating both the Hurricane and one of the world's most lauded drinking spots. Pat O'Brien's was begun by O'Brien in 1933 at the intersection of Royal and St. Peter Streets, but it was probably not his first experience in running a bar. During the days of Prohibition, only a few doors away, was a speakeasy known as Club Tipperary. The Tipperary was only accessed by mumbling the words "storm's brewin,'" and it was allegedly run by Mr. O'Brien — although other accounts claim he discovered and fell in love with New Orleans on his way to Texas after the repeal of the Volstead Act.

If indeed Mr. O'Brien was responsible for the merry making and law breaking at the Tipperary, his supplies would have come via rum-runners. These maverick men would trek a journey of hundreds of miles, crossing from Belize with the contraband. When they came close to the Louisiana shore, they would heave the tins of rum and whiskey into the midnight shallows in sacks. The liquor was retrieved later, after officials had inspected the boats.

In 1933, O'Brien became a legitimate barkeep, and in 1942 he changed addresses with help from his partner Charlie Cantrell to the present location at 718 St. Peter. With the Second World War raging, however, obtaining liquor once again demanded savoir-faire.

Almost every spirit was scarce, whiskey particularly so. The distilleries were converted to make bullets, and the grain was being used to make rations for soldiers. Rum, once as good as gold coins in the purses of pirates, became too much of a good thing for O'Brien and the rest of the city's bartenders. O'Brien and Cantrell began experimenting with the sugary substance, and Fortuna presented herself in the form of a traveling salesman selling glasses modeled after hurricane lanterns. With a heavy-handed pour of rum from Cantrell into O'Brien's concoction of passion fruit juice, lemon juice and sugar — the Hurricane was born. Slightly different versions of the Hurricane were handed out for free to sailors and dockworkers in the beginning days to determine the best taste, and the recipe was finalized in the mid-1940s.

The original courtyard of Pat O'Brien's resembled a lawn more than the patio of today. The building at 718 St. Peter Street dates back to 1791, and it was the location of the first Spanish theater in America.

PAT O'BRIEN
PAT
O'BRIEN'S

Hurricane

Benson Harrison "Pat" O'Brien is credited with creating both the Hurricane and one of the world's most lauded drinking spots. Today, Pat O'Brien's claims to sell more alcohol than any other bar in the world.

The original recipe for Pat O'Brien's Hurricane is a secret. If you want to make the same drink you'll get at Pat O's, you'll need to buy their mix and use this recipe.

Crushed Ice
4 oz. dark rum
4 oz liquid Pat O'Brien's Hurricane Mix®
Orange slice
Maraschino cherry

Fill a 28 ounce Hurricane glass with crushed ice. Add the dark rum and the liquid Hurricane mix to the glass and stir. Garnish with orange slice and maraschino cherry and serve with a straw.

There are many New Orleans bars that have made their own version of the Hurricane. If you want to make a similar drink from scratch, see Lafitte's Blacksmith Shop's recipe for a Pirate's Punch on page 85.

TUJAGUE'S
EST 1856
BAR

TUJAGUE'S

You can prop your foot on the brass foot rail, but that is the only physical relief you will receive besides the liquid in the bottles, stacked amongst the faded tobacco-colored columns and large French mirror on the back bar. Tujague's is New Orleans' oldest stand-up bar. There is no rhyme or reason for the lack of barstools, it has always been that way, with artists, attorneys, politicians and street performers lining up to ease their vastly different worries with a common cocktail at day's end.

In 1852, Guillaume Tujague and his new wife Marie Abadie stepped off the boat from France, and by 1856 the young couple began Tujague's, spending their days feeding dockworkers cold shrimp slathered in homemade remoulade and beef brisket with horseradish.

When the bar and restaurant celebrated its 50th birthday, the sound of carriage whips still cracked as buggies lurched to a start outside. Beer was less than a nickel, and cobblestones were symbols of city advancement.

Shortly before his death in 1912, Guillaume Tujague sold his restaurant to Philbert Guichet, who enlisted the help of a new partner, Jean-Dominic Castet, and in 1914, the two men moved the venerable institution to the corner of Madison and Decatur. It has resided there ever since.

A lure for artists off of Jackson Square, Tujague's ambiance is a conglomeration of artifacts and art collected over the years, most recently by current owner Steven Latter. The table shaped like a painter's palette was left in the 1960s as payment by a starving artist whose thirst was obviously larger than his purse. There is a wine sign on the wall, donated by a woodworker, above Latter's collection of antiquated miniature spirit bottles.

It was Philbert Guichet who designed the recipe for the venue's signature Grasshopper cocktail, which made its first appearance the year after Prohibition was repealed — not that Prohibition mattered much to such an august venue in the first place. During the dry spell from '20 to '33, Guichet still employed three bartenders, valued for their skills at service and surreptitiousness.

Still, the city, and country, struggled in the days directly behind the Volstead Act's demise. It was not established what "sold" a drink. Names, labels, bottle shapes and even drink recipes all had to be reborn in this new era. It was often a bartender's job to be a chemist of sorts, an artist in his own right, painting alcohol's new future. In this way, Tujague's has encouraged the workingman's art, on both sides of the bar, for more than a hundred years.

Left: Photograph of Tujagues' stand-up bar taken at the turn of the 20th Century.

Grasshopper

Around the first or second year following the repeal of Prohibition, a contest was held for the best drink recipe of the new era. At that time, Philbert Guichet had owned Tujague's for more than 10 years, and he traveled to New York City to enter his own creation, The Grasshopper. Guichet won the contest for the city of New Orleans and his proud, old freestanding bar, Tujague's.

Ice cubes
1 oz. green crème de menthe
1 ½ oz. white crème de cacao
¼ oz. brandy
1 oz. light cream
Sprig of mint

Pour all ingredients into a cocktail shaker and shake until mixed and well chilled. Strain into a chilled martini glass and add mint sprig.

Nowhere in America cultivates the sensation of a sip quite like New Orleans. Testimony to this fact is all around, from the advent of the cocktail in egg cups hundreds of years ago to the go cups of today. The city encourages the laissez-faire approach to libation and in the spirit of spirited relaxation, plastic cups are provided and drinks are welcome on the streets.

III

LAST CALL

Remembering and honoring vestiges of history has always been the foundation of this great place. These three pieces of the city are gone. As to whether we as a culture will save them from extinction remains to be seen.

SAZERAC BAR

When the Sazerac Coffee House moved from Exchange Alley to the intersection of Gravier and Carondelet Streets in the earliest days of the 20th century, women were still only allowed inside on Fat Tuesday. Prohibition struck a fatal blow to the profit margins of the Sazerac, and the venue managed to struggle on until 1949 when it finally financially collapsed.

The Roosevelt Hotel came to the rescue and moved the Sazerac to a location on Baronne Street, adjacent to the hotel's golden entrance. The manager in those days was Seymour Weiss, and he welcomed the ladies in permanently, marking the end of a century of sexism.

In the late '50s, the bar moved yet again to space formerly occupied by the Roosevelt's Main Bar. The Main Bar's original trappings were handed down to the gypsy Sazerac, including the 45-foot bar, paneled walls and gorgeous art-deco style backbar. The gleaming amber wood was all carved from the same African walnut tree, and it lends elegance unparalleled by any other establishment in the city. When the Fairmont chain of opulent hotels purchased the Roosevelt in 1965, they were wise to leave the well-respected Sazerac Bar in the lobby.

Before Katrina, patrons flocked in to have a signature sip of the cocktail that lent its name and so much history to the space and to New Orleans overall. Bartenders at The Fairmont were trained, like their Roosevelt predecessors, to spin the glasses into the air to shake free the excess Herbsaint with style, mixing a perfect Sazerac every time.

The Sazerac Bar and its host, The Fairmont, are currently counted among the tally of losses from the storm. Flooding closed the hotel and bar, and there has been no word as to their reopening at this date. It is heartbreaking to contemplate that the city's most honored cocktail, the drink that started it all, has lost its namesake home after all these years.

Artist Paul Ninas painted the mural of New Orleans' street life on the wall of the Art-Deco styled Sazerac Bar in the mid 1930s when the hotel was still known as the Roosevelt. He was nicknamed "The Dean of New Orleans Artists" for his vibrant portrayals in paint.

NICK'S BAR

Nick's Bar has more humorous history than most. Before 1918, the small frame structure was a struggling saloon owned by Nick Castrogiovanni's brother. Nick was having a drink inside on a particularly painful, slow day when his brother proclaimed, "I'm going to sell this place to the next person who walks through that door. For whatever they're willing to pay."

Nick slapped $7.32 on the dusty bar and changed his destiny.

The building's location, directly opposite the Dixie Brewery and just down the street from the train stop for the Baton Rouge line, made it a popular spot for a wide variety of clientele. Nick, however, was oddly paranoid about business. He had a bizarre phobia that the liquor would run low at some point, so he kept a ridiculous back stock. One often-retold legend about Nick's idiosyncrasies involves Hurricane Betsy. When the beast blew into New Orleans in 1965, the roof came down into

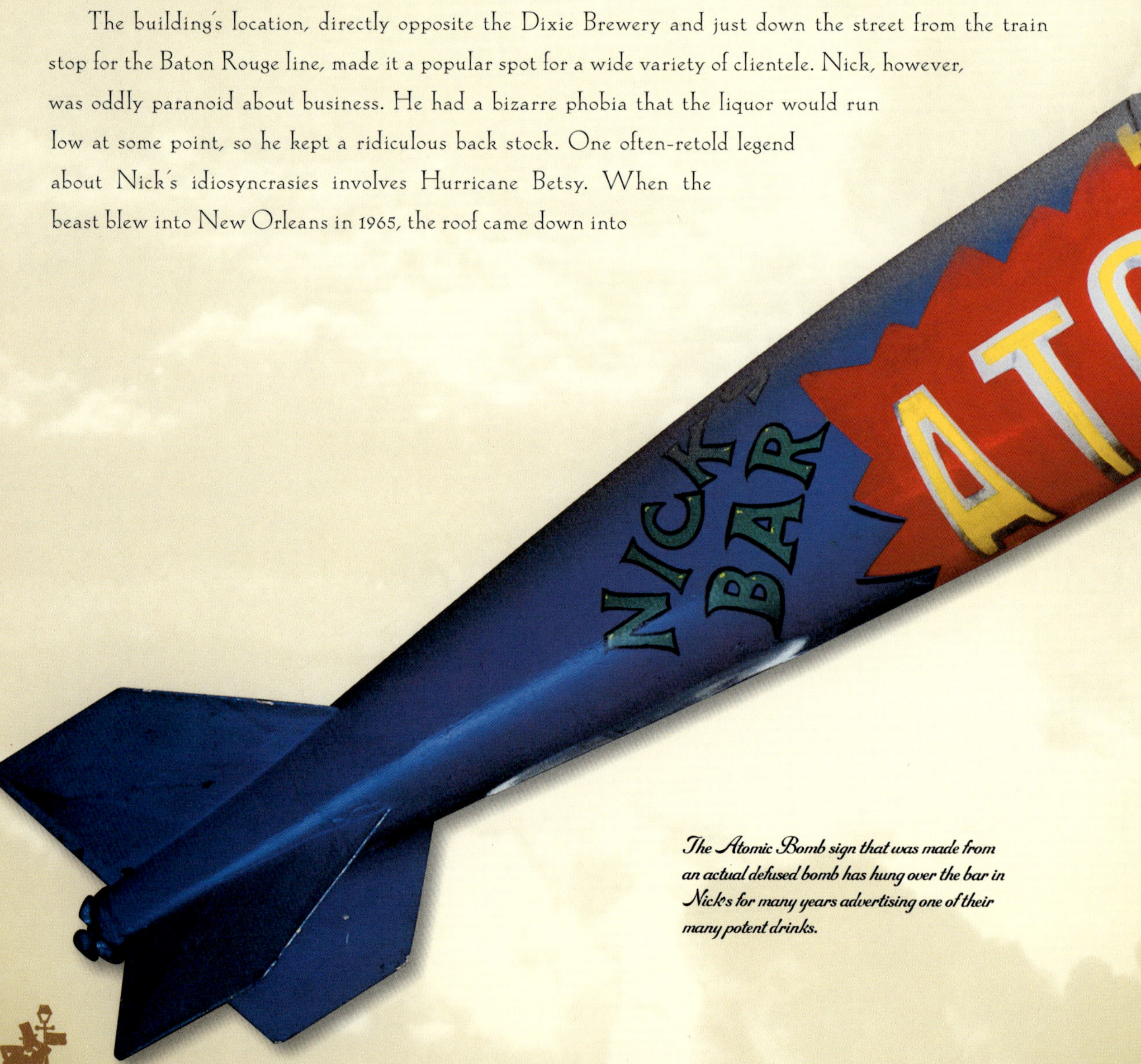

The Atomic Bomb sign that was made from an actual defused bomb has hung over the bar in Nick's for many years advertising one of their many potent drinks.

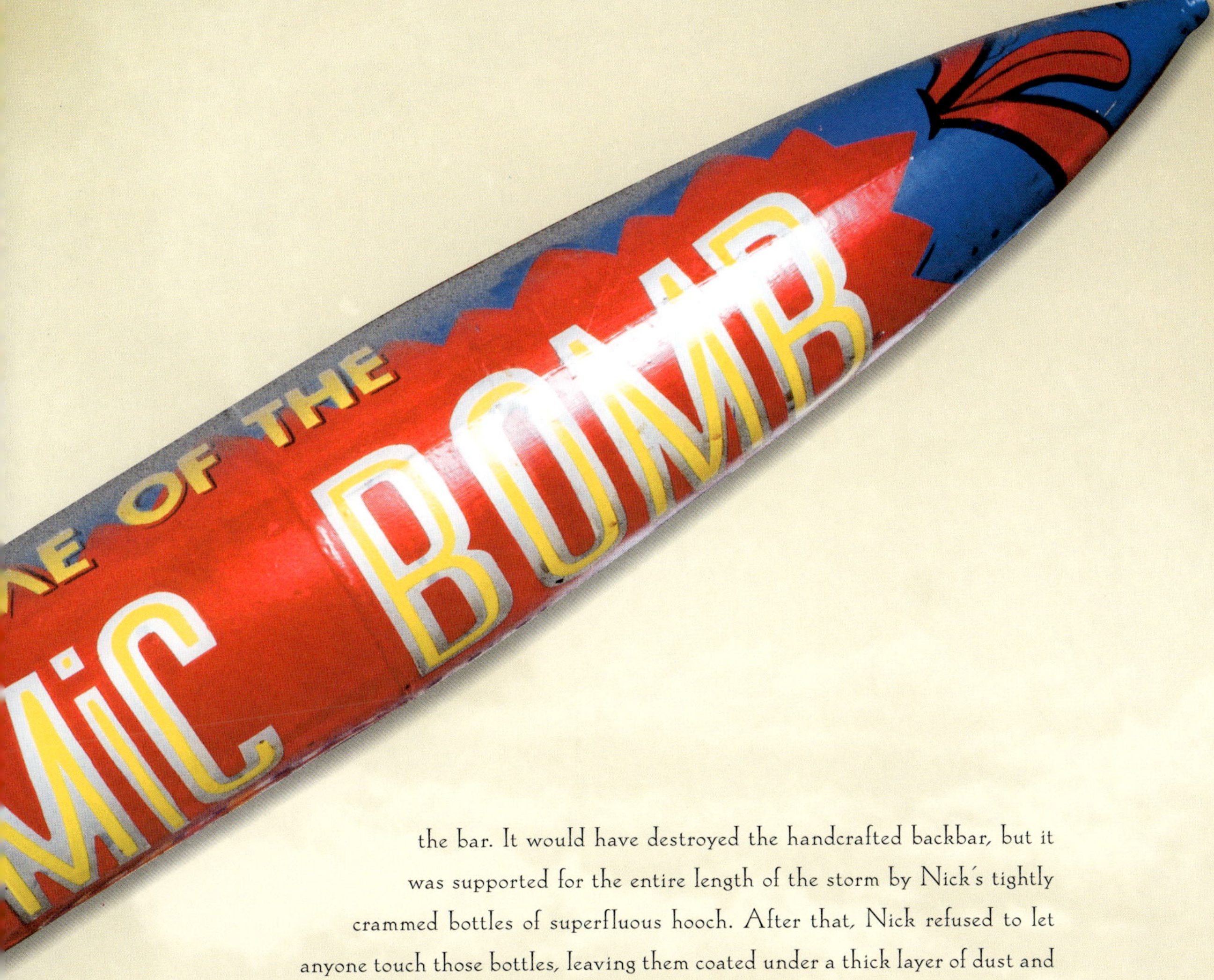

the bar. It would have destroyed the handcrafted backbar, but it was supported for the entire length of the storm by Nick's tightly crammed bottles of superfluous hooch. After that, Nick refused to let anyone touch those bottles, leaving them coated under a thick layer of dust and his own superstition.

Nick was also known for his talent at mixology. He holds the record for shot layering, pouring a 32-layer pousse-café parfait in a 1-ounce shot glass. He won an international mixology competition for 23 consecutive years, and when he died in 1979, America lost one of its premiere masters of the craft. He also left his wife with so many extra bottles that she didn't place a liquor order for years.

Nick's has not reopened since Hurricane Katrina. The locked front door has been kicked in, and the only visible remnants of almost 100 years of business are the bar and the hanging Atomic Bomb sign. If the citizens of New Orleans will one day enjoy the pleasures of a night at Nick's and drinks with names like Pregnant Canary, Sani Flush, Jet Fuel, A Wild Night at the Capri Hotel and Underwater Demolition again remains to be seen.

OLD ABSINTHE BAR SIGN

After Prohibition officials ransacked the interior, friends of The Old Absinthe House, in a declaration of love for past discretions and memories of sweet intoxication, took the marble absinthe fountains, the entire bar and the clock that hung above it and carefully moved them down Bourbon Street to a location that became the Old Absinthe Bar.

People forget the beauty and importance of age in modern times, and in 1998, The Old Absinthe Bar was demolished for the sake of yet another daiquiri shop. The refugee relics disappeared for a while, but they resurfaced eventually inside of Tony Moran's restaurant at the original location of The Old Absinthe House.

The hanging iron sign outside was all that remained of The Old Absinthe Bar. Since Katrina, it has been missing. Sources claim it came down in the high winds of the hurricane and is now stashed in a warehouse until it can be returned to its rightful vantage point. In its absence there is another symbol of what makes New Orleans so undeniable — a reminder that history isn't always aesthetically pleasing or profitable, but the memories that its remaining physical fragments evoke are always beautiful and worth preserving.

This photograph of The Old Absinthe Bar sign was taken in 1997, one year before the bar below it was gutted and turned into the Mango Mango daiquiri shop. The sign remained high above it's Bourbon Street location until it was damaged by the winds of Hurricane Katrina in 2005.

This postcard from the 1930s shows the bar, absinthe fountains and clock from The Old Absinthe House in their new home at The Old Absinthe Bar.

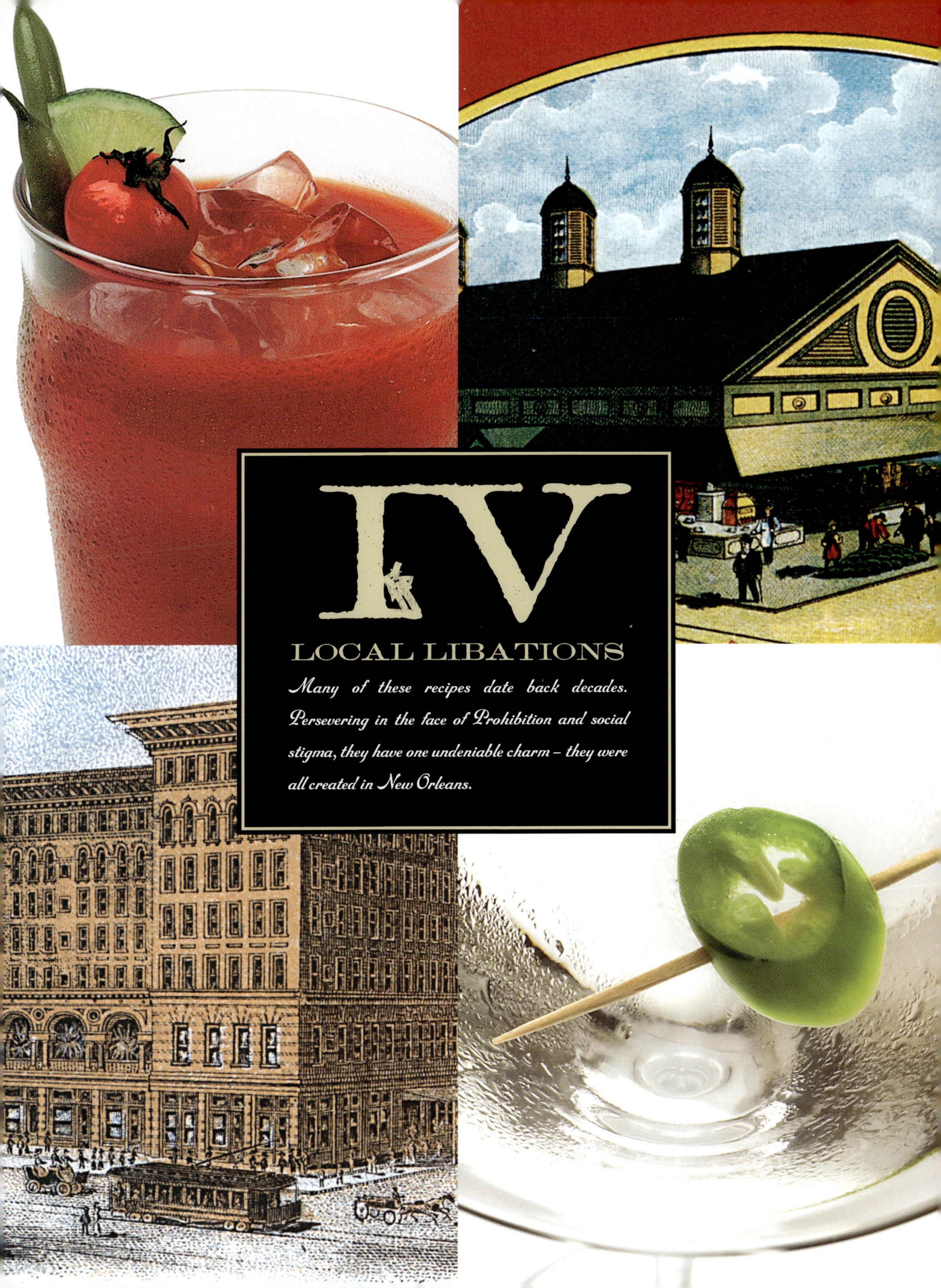

IV

LOCAL LIBATIONS

Many of these recipes date back decades. Persevering in the face of Prohibition and social stigma, they have one undeniable charm – they were all created in New Orleans.

MADE IN U.S.A.
McILHENNY CO.
AVERY ISLAND
LA.
TABASCO®
BRAND
PEPPER SAUCE

TABASCO®

TABASCO® brand Pepper Sauce is an international household name, a Louisiana cooking staple and a vehement after-finish to a multitude of cocktails. The company was begun by Edmund McIlhenny in the 1860s when he planted a few seeds of *Capsicum frutescens* peppers from Mexico or Central America. He grew the peppers in the Avery Island soil in the tropical heat of Southern Louisiana and in 1868, the McIlhenny Company was founded and in full operation. Today the family still owns the company and still produces hot sauce from Avery Island.

A constant spot of character on most tables in American restaurants, the Tabasco label has essentially remained unscathed by marketing ploys for change. Tabasco has more than a century of branding power in its faded tones of red and green.

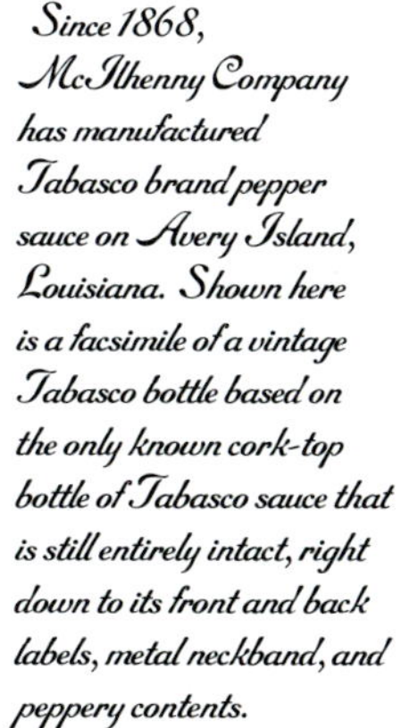

Since 1868, McIlhenny Company has manufactured Tabasco brand pepper sauce on Avery Island, Louisiana. Shown here is a facsimile of a vintage Tabasco bottle based on the only known cork-top bottle of Tabasco sauce that is still entirely intact, right down to its front and back labels, metal neckband, and peppery contents.

Creole Bloody Mary

Ice cubes
1½ oz. vodka
½ tsp. lemon juice
1 pinch of Tony Chacere's® Creole Seasoning
2 to 6 drops Tabasco® brand Pepper Sauce (to taste)
½ cup tomato juice
1 tsp. Worcestershire sauce
Pinch of black pepper
Lime wedge
Spiced green bean
Cherry tomato
Pickled okra pod

Place ice into a large glass, add all ingredients except lime, green bean, cherry tomato and okra pod. Stir well. Squeeze lime wedge into glass. Garnish with green bean, cherry tomato, okra pod as desired.

ST. CHARLES HOTEL

The history of the St. Charles Hotel is a play in three parts. The first St. Charles Hotel was designed by James Gallier, Sr. in the 1840s and was known as the St. Charles Cotton Exchange Hotel. The grand Corinthian columns bordered the avenue, and the dome rose 185 feet, making it a crown for the tallest building in the city at that time.

Fire destroyed the beautiful structure after only nine years of operation, but New Orleanians were not to be denied. The second St. Charles Hotel was erected on the very same site in 1853. The façade was less ornate without the dome, but the inside exceeded most expectations of lavish accommodations. Chandeliers and hot water in the baths were delights of the day, and in a showing of true Southern hospitality, the hotel management provided free lodging for returning Confederate soldiers.

Fire again ravaged the second attempt at extravagance in 1894, and the second St. Charles Hotel suffered so much damage that when the smoke cleared, only the columns remained.

Native architect Thomas Sully was commissioned for the third St. Charles Hotel design, and in 1896, guests were invited back. The space was praised for its beauty in both décor and atmosphere, from the grand staircase in the lobby to the formal functions and private galas. Many citizens were horrified when the hotel was demolished in 1974. The site is now home to a 52-

St. Charles Punch

Ice cubes
1 ½ oz. ruby port
1 oz. Cognac
⅓ oz. caraçao (or Cointreau)
Juice of whole lemon

Put port, Cognac, curaçao, and lemon juice in a tall glass filled with ice and stir. Garnish with a lemon wedge and serve with a straw.

CHICORY COFFEE

Coffee has been a part of New Orleans living since the sun first rose over the newly founded city. The inclination for a morning cup of Joe can be traced as far back as the time when early Acadians made the journey south from Nova Scotia to Louisiana in the late 18th century. Supplies easily spoiled, so trekking pilgrims added roasted endive root to their cargo of coffee to ensure a little bit of the dark-brown bean would go a long way. This was the first "chicory" coffee.

The bitter edge found a sweet spot in Louisiana culture, particularly in New Orleans.

Bars were first known as coffee houses, and coffee remains a staple behind the bar as much as beside the beignets. For an unknown reason, the natives also have a penchant for adding brandy and fire to coffee whenever possible. New Orleans is currently one of the largest coffee importing cities in America.

Cafe Royalé

¾ cup strong chicory coffee, hot
4 tsp. brandy
1 sugar cube

Pour hot chicory coffee into warmed mug. Float 2 teaspoons of brandy on the coffee. Put the remaining 2 teaspoons of brandy into a tablespoon with the sugar cube. Warm the spoon over the hot coffee. With a match, carefully light the brandy in the tablespoon. Slowly lower the spoon into the coffee to ignite the floating brandy. Wait 1 minute after flame has died before drinking.

COUNT ROFFIGNAC

It is undisputed that Joseph Roffignac was one of New Orleans' best mayors. During his term in office from 1820 to 1828 he was responsible for installing the first cobblestones along Royal Street. He also brought the city its first street lighting, its first fire department and its first public educational system.

Roffignac's term included borrowing great sums of money via issuing "city stock." He reinvested the borrowed funds to beautify the city, and one manner in which he did this was the planting of a substantial number of trees around the city. Today, the avenues are cloaked in the shade of his foresight.

In a strange bit of history, both Roffignac and his father, René Annibal de Roffignac, died in remarkable ways. René Annibal was best remembered as a man who gave his life for his country, by offering his own head on the chopping block in place of King Louis XVI. Count Louis Phillippe Joseph de Roffignac was living in France at the time of his own death. He was cleaning his gun and preparing for a return trip to New Orleans when he had an apoplectic stroke. He fell to the floor and the gun discharged. The bullet struck him in the head, killing him instantly.

Roffignac

Crushed Ice
1 oz. Cognac
½ oz. Sazerac Rye®
¾ oz. grenadine (or raspberry syrup)
Fresh raspberries

Pour Cognac, Sazerac Rye, grenadine into an old-fashioned glass filled with crushed ice and stir. Garnish with raspberries.

JOSEPH SANTINA

Like its predecessors and successors in other cocktail categories, the Pousse Café has a murky origin with several recipes claiming to be the sire of the drink that the shooter is based on. Jerry Thomas wrote a book in 1862 entitled *How to Mix Drinks*, and in his section on "Fancy Drinks" there are three recipes for the Pousse Café.

The very first one mentioned in the book is credited to a man named Joseph Santina who operated "Jewel of the South" Saloon next to the St. Charles Hotel. His recipe called for Cognac, Maraschino, and curaço and is widely considered to be the oldest one of the three.

Pousse Café

¼ oz. grenadine
¼ oz. créme de cacao
¼ oz. maraschino liqueur
¼ oz. orange curaçao
¼ oz. green créme de menthe
½ oz. cognac

With a steady hand pour each cordial in the order listed above over the back of a bar spoon angled into a pousse café glass or any small to medium clear glass. The heaviest of the liqueurs are poured in first. The result is colorful layers of liquid that sit on top of each other.

Right: A map of the New Orleans city streets that Count Roffignac had improved and beautified during his term as mayor.

FIRST
MUNICIPALITY
1 2 3 4
PRIEUR
ROMAN
DERBIGNY
CLAIBORNE
ROBERTSON
VILLERE
MARAIS
TREME
FRANKLIN
BASIN
RAMPART
BURGUNDY
DAUPHIN
BOURBON
ROYAL
CHARTRES
OLD LEVEE
CUSTOM HOUSE
BIENVILLE
CONTI
ST. LOUIS
TOULOUSE
ST. PETER
ORLEANS
ST. ANNE
DUMAINE
URSULINES
HOSPITAL
BARRACK
ESPLANADE
EXCHANGE ALLEY
EXCHANGE
CONDE
JEFFERSON
MADISON
PUBLIC SQUARE
MARKET
GALLATIN
CIRCUS PLACE
ST. CLAUDE
PLAUCHE
BAYOU ROAD
CATHOLIC CEMETERY
PALMYRA
JACKSON
POYDRAS
GRAVIER
COMMON
FOUCHER
GOOD CHILDREN
LOVE
BAGATELLE
CRAPS
UNION
GREAT MEN
CASA CALVO
MOREAU
MARIGNY
MANDEVILLE
VICTORY
LEVEE
MORALES
R I V E R
P I
ALGIERS
PATTERSON
PUBLIC PLACE
DELARONDE
PETER
ALIX
ELIZA
EVELINA
OCTAVIA
BIENVENU
HELEN
CHURCH
FERRY
HOMER
NEWTON
DECATUR
DE ARMAS
LA PEROUSE
SEGUIN
BOUIS
BARTHOLOMEW
LA VERGNE
VERRET

PAUL PRUDHOMME

Renowned Chef Paul Prudhomme has given the city multitudes of recipes and recognition. The recipe for the Cajun Martini has found a sweet, albeit spicy, spot in the heart of natives. The drink was invented by Chef Paul Prudhomme and his late wife Kay in their restaurant, K-Paul's Kitchen, and it takes a little more time to prepare because of the infusion process. All great things, the Martini included, are made better with time.

Cajun Martini

You can make this recipe with commercially prepared pepper vodka or you can make your own pepper vodka or gin. Wash 3 jalapeno peppers. Gently puncture or slice the peppers so the alcohol will be able to be infused with the peppers' flavors. Put the peppers in a quart of vodka or gin and refrigerate for at least 3 days. If refrigerated for more than a week the alcohol must be strained before use.

Ice cubes
5 oz. pepper infused vodka or gin
Dry vermouth
1 small jalapeno or a pickled mirliton

Fill a shaker with ice and add the pepper infused alcohol and shake well. Then strain into a chilled large martini glass that has been slightly rinsed or misted with vermoth and garnish with jalapeno slice or mirliton slice.

OLD
NEW
ORLEANS
750 ML 40% ALC/VOL
(80 PROOF)
CRYSTAL
LOUISIANA
RUM

OLD NEW ORLEANS RUM

A place of pirates and plunder, it's only natural for the city to have its own rum brand. "A marvelous mixer, a Louisiana elixir" is the tag line for the locally produced Old New Orleans Rum. The spirit is made with the same festive attitude characteristic of those rums hailing from The Caribbean — only the Mississippi River soil and Louisiana sugar cane lend a splendid taste of home.

The rums produced are all handcrafted, small-batch premium artisan blends made exclusively with this Southern state's sugar cane crops. While the label goes through the occasional change, the product within is held to strict standards. Lending itself to easy consumption straight up or mixed, the company has developed a recipe suggested for drinkers. It is only right that it be named after a New Orleans' staple such as the party-friendly Frenchmen Street.

The Frenchmen

Ice cubes
1 ½ oz. Old New Orleans Crystal Rum®
½ oz. peach schnapps
½ oz. sour mix
½ oz. cranberry juice

Combine all ingredients in a shaker with ice. Shake well and serve straught up or on the rocks.

Left and above: Oak barrels containing Old New Orleans Rum at Celebration Distillation on Frenchmen Street.

ABSOLUT® NEW ORLEANS

In August 2007, The Absolut Spirits Company will bring a special form of hurricane aid to the states of Louisiana, Alabama and Mississippi via the vehicle it knows best — vodka. The company is releasing a limited-edition flavor entitled ABSOLUT® NEW ORLEANS, which will be available nationwide in bars, restaurants, hotels, nightclubs and retail locations. The flavor profile is a fruity mango vodka with a spicy black pepper kick. The company also is a platinum sponsor of Tales of the Cocktail 2007 in New Orleans, and lucky attendees to the festival will be welcomed with the ABSOLUT BIG BREEZY signature cocktail before anyone else. The official unveiling of the vodka and its signature cocktail will be held at a press conference on July 18th, the first day of this prestigious culinary and cocktail festival. This drink was designed to highlight the unique, local flavors of ABSOLUT NEW ORLEANS. With each sip, guests will be helping with the relief efforts in a sense of spirit and celebration.

One hundred percent of The Absolut Spirits Company's net profits of this product will be donated to charities helping the regions affected by Hurricane Katrina. These include the Tipitina's Foundation, the Louisiana Restaurant Association and Volunteer Mobile, among others.

ABSOLUT® Big Breezy

4-5 chunks of fresh watermelon
2 oz. Absolut® New Orleans
½ oz. simple syrup
Squeeze of lemon
Pinch of black pepper

Shake and strain ingredients into a martini glass and garnish with a melon ball and lemon slice and pinch of black pepper.

DALTON MILTON

This innovation on a classic Martini was developed to honor a very special French Quarter character. Dalton Milton was a legend when he retired in 2007 from his position of maitre'd of the Rib Room located in the Omni Royal Orleans on the corner of Royal and St. Louis Streets.

A graduate of Joseph S. Clark High School in New Orleans, Dalton was hired in 1961 as a busboy for a salary of $18 a week when the location was still known as the French Quarter Hotel and Restaurant. He then worked as a cocktail waiter at the hotel's rooftop Le Riviera venue and by 1967, he had been promoted to waiter. Several more promotions followed until Dalton became the restaurant's manager in 1996.

In his final position of maitre'd, Dalton could easily tell his patrons — often known politicians, celebrities and socialites — five decades of stories from his time in one of the city's most upscale places to dine and drink. Upon his retirement this recipe for the Dalton Miltini was added to the permanent menu at the Rib Room. It is his personal favorite libation.

Dalton Miltini

Ice
2 oz. Chopin Vodka® (kept in the freezer and extra chilled)
1/2 oz. Cinzano Dry Vermouth®
Pinch of sea salt
3 pimento stuffed queen olives

Shake first 4 ingredients with ice and strain into a martini glass. Garnish with three queen olives stuffed with pimento.

MARVIN ALLEN

Marvin Allen has been involved in the food and beverage industry for over 35 years. For the past 5 of these years he has been the head bartender at the Carousel Piano Bar and Lounge at the Hotel Monteleone. Marvin enjoys blending a variety of flavors into new cocktail creations. The recipe below was a winner in the 2004 Tales of the Cocktail drink contest.

Southern Comfortini

Ice
1 ¼ oz. Southern Comfort®
1 ¼ oz. peach schnapps
1 ¼ oz. black raspberry liquor
1 ¼ oz. pineapple juice
Squeeze of fresh lemon juice
Lemon twist

Place first 6 ingredients in a cocktail shaker with ice. Shake until frothy and well chilled. Strain into a cocktail glass and garnish with lemon twist.

1960's postcard of original Carousel Bar in the Hotel Monteleone.

Photograph of a typical night at the city's ultimate dive, the Saturn Bar on St. Claude Avenue in 1996. The eclectic bar that was owned and operated by the late O'Neil Broyard for over 40 years was severly damaged by Hurricane Katrina, but has since reopened at it's Bywater location.

APPENDIX

Bibliography

A Guide to the Historic Shops and Restaurants of New Orleans. New York: The Little Bookroom, 2004.

Arthur, Stanley Clisby. *Famous New Orleans Drinks and How to Mix'em.* Gretna: Pelican Publishing Company, 2000.

Bailey, Mark. *Hemingway and Bailey's Bartending Guide to Great American Writers.* Chapel Hill: Algonquin Books of Chapel Hill, 2006.

Bannos, Jimmy, and John DeMers. *Big Easy Cocktails: Jazzy Drinks and Savory Bites from New Orleans.* Berkeley: Ten Speed Press, 2006.

Benson, Jyl, and Melvin Rodrigue. *Galatoire's Cookbook.* New York: Clarkson Potter/ Publishers, 2005.

Boulard, Garry. *Huey Long Invades New Orleans: The Siege of a City, 1934-36.* Gretna: Pelican Publishing Company, 1998.

Brennan, Jimmy, Pip and Ted. *Breakfast at Brennan's, and Dinner Too.* New Orleans: Brennan's Inc., 1994.

Collier, Phillip, and J. Richard Gruber, Jim Rapier, Mary Beth Romig. *Missing New Orleans.* New Orleans: The Ogden Museum of Southern Art, Inc., 2005.

Conrad, Barnaby. *Absinthe: History in a Bottle.* San Francisco: Chronicle Books, 1988.

Guste, Roy F. Jr. *Antoine's Restaurant since 1840: Cookbook.* New Orleans: Guste Publishing, 1979.

Heard, Malcolm. *French Quarter Manual: An Architectural Guide to New Orleans' Vieux Carre*. New Orleans: Tulane School of Architecture, 1997.

Hermesch, Robert, and Betina J. Wittels. *Absinthe: Sip of Seduction*. Denver: Speck Press, 2003.

Huber, Leonard V. *New Orleans: A Pictorial History*. Gretna: Pelican Publishing Company, 1991.

Macchione, Mikko. *Napoleon House*. New Orleans: Cheers Publishing L.L.C, 2006.

McCaffety, Kerri. *Obituary Cocktail: The Great Saloons of New Orleans*. New Orleans: Winter Books, 1998.

Picayune Creole Cook Book. New Orleans: The Times Picayune Publishing Co., 1901.

Wohl, Kit. *Arnaud's Restaurant Cookbook: New Orleans Legendary Creole Cuisine*. Gretna: Pelican Publishing Company, 2005.

www.antoines.com
www.antoinescookbook.com
www.bestofneworleans.com
www.brennansneworleans.com
www.cocktailtimes.com
www.corpse.org
www.epicurious.com
www.experienceneworleans.com
www.frenchquarter.com
www.margaritaville.com
www.oldabsinthehouse.com
www.oxygenee.com
www.patobriens.com
www.pbs.org
www.pharmacymuseum.org
www.practicallyedible.com
www.roffignac.com
www.thecolumns.com
www.tujaguerestaurant.com
www.ukbg.co.uk
www.woodlandplantation.com

Friends & Selected Websites

Antoine's Restaurant
www.antoines.com
World renowned for it's French Creole cuisine, service, and atmosphere, Antoine's has set the standard for all other restaurants in New Orleans since 1840.

Arnaud's Restaurant
www.arnauds.com
This restaurant is the 85 year old French Quarter's "Grand Dame" that serves classic Creole cuisine. Their brunch, with a background of traditional New Orleans jazz, is not to be missed.

Brennan's Restaurant
www.brennansneworleans.com
Have your most important meal of the day at the most famous breakfast restaurant in the world. This New Orleans institution has 15 "eye-openers" on the menu.

The Columns Hotel
www.thecolumns.com
A grand hotel on St. Charles Avenue in the Upper Garden district of New Orleans. It's large front porch or the Victorian Lounge is a great place to have late afternoon drinks.

Galatoire's Restaurant
www.galatoires.com
For over a hundred years Galatoire's has been the New Orleans favorite old-line restaurant where "lunch hours become lunch afternoons."

The Historic New Orleans Collection
www.hnoc.org
A great place to do research, this collection contains over 35,000 library items and more than 300,000 photographs, prints, drawings, and paintings of New Orleans history.

The Hotel Monteleone
www.hotelmonteleone.com
This fourth generation family owned hotel is the French Quarter's oldest and most opulent hotel. Sit in the Carousel Bar and imagine Tennessee Williams or Truman Capote sitting on the stool next to you.

La Maison d'Absinthe
www.lamaisondabsinthe.com
This New Orleans owned company has the best website in America for Absinthe fountains, spoons, and glasses for customers preferring the traditional, pre-ban French and Swiss methods of drinking absinthe.

The Library of Congress
www.loc.gov
The American Memory section of this website is a prodigious digital record that documents the words, recordings, images, prints, maps, and sheet music of American history.

The Louisiana State Museum
http://lsm.crt.state.la.us
This museum is a complex of national landmarks in New Orleans housing thousands of artifacts and works of art reflecting Louisiana history.

Mark Andresen
www.markandresenillustration.com
This versatile and talented artist was forced to relocate to Atlanta due to Hurricane Katrina. Mark created the drunk man icon that is used throughout this book.

Martha Torres
www.newstyling.com
Martha does incredible food styling and production designing for food and beverage clients. She styled many of the drink photographs in this book.

Michael Terranova
www.terranovaphoto.com
Visit this site and view beautiful photographs of New Orleans people, places, and cuisine by the photographer of this book.

Museum of the American Cocktail
www.museumoftheamericancocktail.org
This website leads visitors through the fascinating two hundred year history of the American cocktail.

Mignon Faget
www.mignonfaget.com
On this website you will find an extraordinary line of glassware etched with New Orleans icons by Mignon Faget, a highly acclaimed artist and local designer of jewelry.

The Napoleon House
www.napoleonhouse.com
New Orleans' 200 year old landmark bar is my personal favorite and maybe the best bar in America as said by Esquire magazine in 2006.

New Orleans Tourism Marketing Corporation
www.neworleansonline.com
The city's official and by far the best web site for hotel reservations, restaurants, and what to do and see in New Orleans.

The New Orleans Museum of Art
www.noma.org
Visit this museum located in City Park that has a magnificent collection of more than 40,000 art objects and take a stroll outdoors through one of the most important and beautiful sculpture installations in the country.

The New Orleans Public Library
www.nutrias.org
The Special Collections section has thousands of rare maps, menus, postcards, books, and manuscripts pertaining to the history of New Orleans. Please go to the Rebuild section on this website to help repair the libraries destroyed by Hurricane Katrina.

The Ogden Museum of Southern Art
www.ogdenmuseum.org
You'll discover "the portal to Southern culture" at this New Orleans museum. It's the largest and most comprehensive collection of Southern art in the world.

Old Absinthe House
www.oldabsinthehouse.com
Sit at the bar and order an Absinthe Frappé, maybe 2 or 3 and have an imaginary conversation with Oscar Wilde or Aleister Crowley

Old New Orleans Rum
www.oldneworleansrum.com
These award winning rums are made with Louisiana sugar cane at a distillery housed in an old cotton warehouse in New Orleans.

Pat O'Brien's
www.patobriens.com
Pat O's is the originator of the Hurricane and the ultimate party bar in New Orleans. I promise you will "have fun."

Phillip Collier Designs
www.phillipcollierdesigns.com &
www.missingneworleans.com
Please visit these "in progress websites" for my graphic design studio and my book *Phillip Collier's Missing New Orleans*, published by the Ogden Museum of Southern Art in 2005. And remember "the cobbler's children have no shoes."

Roffignac Cognac
www.roffignac.com
This website gives information about the vineyards, distillery, castle, and cellars of the Count de Roffignac near Cognac, France. The owners are the descendants of the Count Roffignac, mayor of New Orleans in the early 1800's.

The Sazerac Company
www.sazerac.com
This New Orleans family owned company dates back to 1850 and is the distiller and distributor of the "Holy Trinity" of New Orleans spirits: Sazerac Rye, Peychaud's Bitters, and Herbsaint.

Southern Comfort
www.southerncomfort.com
Check out SoCo's website and click the "Southern Comfort Music Fund" for an excellent way for you to play a part in the restoration and rebirth of New Orleans by helping musicians get back on their feet and back on stage.

Southern Food and Beverage Museum
www.southernfood.org
Pull up your chair and dig in to a gastronomic temple dedicated to the discovery, understanding, and celebration of the culture of food and drink in the South.

Tabasco
www.tabasco.com
If you think Tabasco only makes pepper sauce, check out this fun website to see the myriad of products they make under their brand name.

Tales of the Cocktail
www.TalesoftheCocktail.com
A culinary and cocktail festival which allows the connoisseur or amateur to fully experience cocktail culture in New Orleans and around the world as presented by the country's hottest chefs, authors, bartenders and cocktail experts. Tales of the Cocktail has "shaken and stirred" the New Orleans French Quarter since 2003.

Tujaques
www.tujaguesrestaurant.com
It's the city's second oldest restaurant and serves traditional New Orleans Creole dishes. Stand at New Orleans' oldest freestanding bar and take a trip back to another era.

Wayne Curtis
www.waynecurtis.com
This New Orleans based writer of stories on travel, architecture, and history was named the Lowell Thomas Travel Journalist of the Year in 2002. His bio is a must read.

Authors

Phillip Collier was born in Wetumpka, Alabama and grew up in nearby Montgomery. He earned a B.F.A. in visual design from Auburn University. After working in Birmingham for a short time, he moved to New Orleans in 1975 to work as a freelance illustrator, art and creative director, before establishing his own firm, Phillip Collier Designs, in 1990. Local clients include Arthur Roger Gallery, The Hotel Monteleone, Louisiana Philharmonic Orchestra, Mignon Faget, The National WWII Museum, New Orleans Museum of Art, New Orleans Tourism Marketing Corp. and the Ogden Museum of Southern Art. National clients have included the Palmer House Hotel (Chicago), the Waldorf Astoria (New York), CBS Sports Radio, Sprint and TABASCO. Collier has won many local, regional and national design awards and was selected to create the official poster of the 1980 Jazz and Heritage Festival, which was chosen for the cover of the *Library of Congress Quarterly* magazine and was included in the Library of Congress' 100-year Retrospective on the History of Posters. His book *Phillip Collier's Missing New Orleans* was at the printer in New Orleans when Hurricane Katrina struck on Augest 29, 2005. The book, published by the Ogden Museum of Southern Art, was still miraculously printed in the storm ravaged city just three months after the hurricane.

Jennifer Adams is a graduate of the College of Charleston who has worked as an associate editor for *Nightclub & Bar* magazine. She is a frequent freelance contributor to *Executive Traveler, Portico and Delta* magazines. Jennifer also contributes a monthly cocktail column entitled "Hip to Sip" to Greater New Orleans Living magazine. She enjoys traveling, live music and returning to New Orleans whenever possible.

Michael Terranova is a self taught photographer, who started his freelance career here in New Orleans in 1981. Besides a thriving commercial business, Terranova has also enjoyed a successful editorial career, having been published in *Bon Appetit, Food & Wine* and *Wine Spectator* magazines just to name a few. His love of the city is reflected in the many dramatic photos of The French Quarter which have been used to promote the city, through his work with the New Orleans Tourism Marketing Corp.

Illustration detail from 1948 advertisement for the Beverly Country Club, New Orleans. The Beverly was a posh roadhouse club that opened in 1945 and was supposedly owned in a joint venture between the New York and New Orleans Mafia. The dining, drinking, dancing, and gambling lasted only six years. In 1951, federal agents came to town and shut the doors on the River Road establishment due to tax evasion.

Credits

All reasonable efforts have been made to trace the copyright holders of the visual material reproduced herein. We apologize to anyone who has not been reached.

Cover Top: Mint Julep and shaker photograph by Michael Terranova.
Cover Bottom: Court of Two Sisters photograph, The Historic New Orleans Collection, accession no. 1974.25.2.68
Inside front cover: Ramos Gin Fizz advertisement, courtesy of the Fairmont Hotel, New Orleans
Page 2: photograph by Michael Terranova
Page 4: Absinthe Bar Advertisement, collection of the author
Pages 6 and 7: *Absinthe House, New Orleans*, 26' x 32', oil on canvas, courtesy of the regis Corporation, Minneapolis, MN
Pages 8 and 9: Barroom Interior, West End, by George Francis Mungier, from the collection of the Louisiana State Museum, no 09813.575.1
Page 10: Tujague's photograph courtesy of Steve Latter
Page 13: Galatoire's photographs by Michael Terranova
Page 14: poster, courtesy of the New Orleans Pharmacy Museum
Pages 16 and 17: women in Sazerac Bar photograph, courtesy of the Fairmont Hotel, New Orleans
Page 18: absinthe topette photograph by Michael Terranova, absinthe topette courtesy of Cary Bonnecaze
Page 19: details clockwise from top left; Manhattan cockatil photograph - Michael Terranova, Huey Long photograph - Louisiana State Library, Sazerac cocktail photograph - Michael Terranova, poster - Library of Congress
Page 20: Pharmacy Museum photograph by Michael Terranova
Page 21:437 Royal Street photograph, The Historic New Orleans Collection, accession no. VCS Sq63. Egg Cup photograph by Michael Terranova, egg cup courtesy of New Orleans Pharmacy Museum
Page 22: Peychaud Manhattan photograph by Michael Terranova, stylist Martha Torres
Page 23: Peychaud bottles photograph by Michael Terranova
Page 24: Sazerac photograph by Michael Terranova
Page 25: Sazerac menu, courtesy of Stanley Schwan, Sazerac Co. and Lane Casteix, SPAR, Inc. Exchange Alley photograph, courtesy of the New Orleans Public Library
Pages 26 and 27: Sazerac bar photograph, The Historic New Orleans Collection, accession no. 1974.25.2.72
Page 28: Sazerac Rye photograph by Michael Terranova
Page 29: Sazerac cocktail photograph by Michael Terranova, stylist Martha Torres
Page 30: Southern Comfort bottle photograph by Michael Terranova
Page 32: Woodland Plantation engraving by Alfred Waud from Every Saturday magazine, May 20, 1871, The Historic New Orleans Collection, accession no. 1974.25.26.172
Page 33: Scarlett O'Hara cocktail photograph by Michael Terranova, Fleur de Lis tumbler, courtesy of Mignon Faget
Page 34: Pernod poster, courtesy of the Library of Congress
Page 35: Pernod bottle photograph by Michael Terranova. Wormwood farmers postcard and Pernod Absinthe bottle, courtesy of Cary Bonnecaze
Page 36: Label photograph by Michael Terranova. New Orleans Absinthe label, courtesy of B.J. Bordelon III.
Page 37: bottle photograph by Michael Terranova. New Orleans absinthe bottle, courtesy of B.J. Bordelon III
Page 38: Legenedre bottle photograph by Michael Terranova. Legendre Herbsaint bottle, courtesy of Stanley Schwan, Sazerac Co. and Lane Casteix, SPAR, Inc.
Page 39: Absinthe fountain photograph by Michael Terranova
Pages 40 and 41: Absinthe House photograph, The Historic New Orleans Collection, accession no. 1974.25.2.61
Page 42: Absinthe Frappe photograph by Michael Terranova, stylist Martha Torres
Page 43: Herbsaint bottle photograph by Michael Terranova
Page 44: Ramos Gin Fizz recipe book, the Historic New Orleans Collection, accession no. 95-369-RL
Page 45: Meyers Restaurant photograph, The Historic New Orleans Collection, accession no. 81-1082-RL. Henry C. Ramos photograph, the Historic New Orleans Collection, accession no. 1981.305.60iv
Page 46: Huey Long photograph, State Library of Louisiana, object file name hp001023
Page 47: Ramos Gin Fizz cocktail photograph by Michael Terranova
Page 48: New Orleans drunk man souvenir photograph by Michael Terranova
Page 49: details clockwise from top left; Count Arnaud - Arnaud's Restaurant, Grasshopper cocktail photograph - Michael Terranova, Napoleon House bar - Michael Terranova, Vieux Carre Cocktail - Michael Terranova
Page 50: Antoines postcard, courtesy of Mona Mia Antiques
Page 51: Antoines painting, courtesy of Colette Guste, Antoine's Restaurant. Harper's Weekly illustration, The Historic New Orleans Collection, accession no. 1980.110
Page 52: Menu cover and drawing, courtesy of Colette Guste, Antoine's Restaurant
Page 53: Antoine's waiter photograph by Michael Terranova
Page 54: Waiter making Café Brulôt photograph by Michael Terranova
Page 55: Café Brulôt photograph by Michael Terranova, stylist Martha Torres
Page 56: Arnaud's entrance photograph by Michael Terranova
Page 57: French 75 Bar photograph by Michael Terranova
Page 58: French 75 cocktail photograph by Michael Terranova
Page 59: Count Arnaud photograph, courtesy of Arnaud's Restaurant
Page 60: Mimosa photograph by Michael Terranova
Page 61: Brennan's menu cover, courtesy of Ellen and Ted Brennan
Page 62: Mimosa photograph by Michael Terranova
Page 63: Owen Brennan photograph, courtesy of Ellen and Ted Brennan
Page 64: Carousel Bar photograph by Michael Terranova
Page 65: Carousel Bar illustration and postcard, courtesy of the Hotel Monteleone

Page 66: Vieux Carre cocktail photograph by Michael Terranova
Page 67: Carousel photograph by Michael Terranova
Page 68: Truman Capote photograph by Carl Van Vechten, 1948,
Library of Congress, Prints & Photographs Division, Carl Van Vechten
Collection, (reproduction number, e.g. LC-USZ62-54231)
Page 69: Screwdriver cocktail photograph by Michael Terranova
Page 70: Columns exterior photograph by Michael Terranova
Page 71: Raleigh Rye bottle from advertisement in the *Blue Book*,
The Historic New Orleans Collection
Pages 72 and 73: Columns Bar photograph by Michael Terranova
Page 74: Untitled (Women Playing Cards) circa 1912, E.J. Bellocq,
courtesy of the New Orleans Museum of Art, no. 73.240
Page 75: Bellocq photograph, Tulane University Library, Lousiana collection.
Pretty Baby cocktail photograph by Michael Terranova, stylist Martha Torres
Page 76: Galatoire's window photograph by Michael Terranova
Page 77: Galatoire's postcard, The Historic New Orleans Collection,
accession no.1990.20.4.
Page 78: Ojen cocktail photograph by Michael Terranova
Page 79: Galatoire's waiters photograph by Michael Terranova
Page 80: Brandy Alexander photograph by Michael Terrranova.
Tennessee Williams letter, courtesy of Faulkner House Books
Page 81: Tennessee Williams photograph, The
Historic New Orleans Collection, accession no. 2003.228.1 f.4
Page 82: Lafitte's Blacksmith Shop exterior photograph
by Michael Terranova
Page 83: Lafitte's Blacksmith Shop postcard, the Historic
New Orleans Collection, accession no. 1990.20.4.
Lafitte's lantern photograph by Michael Terranova
Page 84: Lafitte portrait photograph by Michael Terranova
Page 85: Pirate's Punch cocktail photograph by Michael Terranova,
stylist Martha Torres
Page 86: Napoleon House bar photograph by Michael Terranova
Page 87: Napoleon House postcard, The Historic New Orleans Collection,
accession no. 1974.25.41.120. Napoleon House sign photograph
by Michael Terranova
Pages 88 and 89: Pimm's Cup cocktail photograph by Michael Terranova,
stylist Martha Torres. Rooftop photograph by Michael Terranova
Page 90: New Orleans Athletic Club bar photograph by Michael Terranova
Page 91: John L. Sullivan drawing, courtesy of New Orleans Athletic Club
Page 92: William Faulkner photograph by Carl Van Vechten, 1948,
Library of Congress, Prints & Photographs Division, Carl Van Vechten
Collection, (reproduction number, e.g. LC-DIG-ppmsca-10445)
Page 93: Mint Julep photograph by Michael Terranova
Page 94: Old Absinthe House wall photograph by Michael Terranova
Page 95: Absinthe House postcard, courtesy of Mona Mia Antiques.
Absinthe Fountain photograph by Michael Terranova
Pages 96 and 97: Absinthe House photograph by C.F. Weber,
courtesy of Joe Bergeron, Bergeron Gallery
Page 98: Entresol photograph by Michael Terranova
Page 99: Absinthe House sign photograph, courtesy of Ellen
and Ted Brennan

Page 100: Hurricanes photograph by Michael Terranova
Page 101: Pat O'Briens coaster, courtesy of Al Kleindienst.
Pat O'Briens courtyard postcard, the Historic New Orleans Collection,
accession no. 1958.85.179
Page 102: Pat O'Brien's exterior photograph by Michael Terranova
Page 103: Hurricane cocktail photograph by Michael Terranova,
stylist Martha Torres
Page 104: Tujague's exterior photograph by Michael Terranova
Page 105: Tujague's bottle photograph by Michael Terranova.
Bottle courtesy of Steve Latter
Page 106: Tujague's photograph, courtesy of Steve Latter
Page 107: Grasshopper cocktail photograph by Michael Terranova
Page 108: Go-cups photograph by Michael Terranova
Page 109: details clockwise from top left; Absinthe bar postcard -
collection of the author, Sazerac bar mural – Michael Terranova, Absinthe
Bar sign - Michael Terranova, Sazerac bartender - Michael Terranova
Page 110: Sazerac Bar photograph by Michael Terranova
Page 111: Roosevelt Hotel postcard, courtesy of Mona Mia Antiques
Pages 112 and 113: Sazerac Bar photograph by Michael Terranova
Pages 114 and 115: Atomic Bomb sign photograph by Michael Terranova
Pages 116 and 117: Absinthe Bar sign photograph by Michael Terranova
Page 118: Absinthe Bar postcard, from the collection of the author
Page 119: details clockwise from top left; Creole Bloody Mary photograph
- Michael Terranova, French Market coffee label - Historic New Orleans
Collection, Cajun Martini cocktail photograph - Michael Terranova,
St. Charles Hotel letterhead - collection of the author
Page 120: Tabasco label, courtesy of The McIlhenny Co.
Page 121: Vintage Tabasco bottle, courtesy of The McIlhenny Co.,
Creole Bloody Mary cocktail photography by Michael Terranova, stylist
Martha Torres
Page 122: St. Charles Hotel postcard, from the collection of the author
Page 123: French Market coffee label,
Historic New Orleans Collection, accession no. 1979.378.3
Page 124: French Quarter map, The Library of Congress
Page 125: Pousse Café photograph by Michael Terranova
Pages 126 and 127: Cajun Martini photograph by Michael Terranova
Page 128: Rum bottles photograph by Michael Terranova
Page 129: Rum factory photographs by Michael Terranova
Page 130: Absolut bottle photograph by Michael Terranova
Page 131: Carousel Bar postcard courtesy of the Hotel Monteleone
Page 132, 133: Saturn Bar photograph by Michael Terranova
Page 135: Martini Sazerac Cocktail bottle, photography by
Michael Terranova, courtesy of Steve Latter
Page 139: Illustration from Beverly Country Club advertisement,
collection of the author
Inside back cover: Ramos Gin Fizz advertisement, courtesy of the
Fairmont Hotel, New Orleans
Back Cover: Absinthe glass photograph by Michael Terranova,
courtesy of Cary Bonnecaze

Index

SOME DRINKING HINTS OF 50 YEARS AGO

I

Take a large tablespoon of good Olive Oil before the party starts and your stomach will be well prepared for what is to follow.

II

Peanuts will do most toward sweetening your breath when it becomes too powerful.

III

If your head begins to swim – a good strong cup of black coffee will help you wonderfully. If you need something stronger – take a tablespoonful of bi-carbonate of soda and a dash of aromatic spirits of ammonia in a tumbler filled with charged water and toss it down – you'll get sober quickly!

IV

If you feel weakish when you get home after a party take a glass of warm milk with sugar in it just before you go to bed. You'll be glad in the morning that you did.

V

Never try to imitate a reservoir – you can't hold all there is. Move around at a party – don't just sit and drink. Have a good time – laugh, dance, and even sing. The more exercise you take the better you can stand the gaff.

The above was taken from a drink recipe book for Legendre Herbsaint published in 1934.